First edition for North America and the Philippines
published in 2015 by Barron's Educational Series, Inc.

Copyright 2015 © RotoVision SA, Sheridan House, 114
Western Road, Hove, East Sussex BN3 1DD, England

All inquiries should be addressed to:
Barron's Educational Series, Inc.
250 Wireless Boulevard
Hauppauge, New York 11788
www.barronseduc.com

Commissioning Editor: Isheeta Mustafi
Editor: Angela Koo
Assistant Editor: Tamsin Richardson
Technical Reader: Nicole Vasbinder
Art Director: Lucy Smith
Design and layout: Lucy Smith and Michelle Rowlandson
Cover design: Lucy Smith
Illustrator: Sarah Lawrence

ISBN: 978-1-4380-0540-9

Library of Congress Control Number: 2014942341

Printed in China

9 8 7 6 5 4 3 2 1

Cover image credits
Front cover (clockwise from top left): Terry jersey dress by
Nancy Dee Brooke; Skirt made in Marc Jacobs cotton poplin by
Lauren Taylor; Floral dress by Free People, styled by Kayley Anne;
Floral pleated skirt by La Redoute; Patterned dress by BHS; Print
dress by Dressabelle, styled by Uli Chan.
Back cover (from left to right): Vintage leather skirt, styled by
Emily Lane; Button up dress by La Redoute; Babydoll dress by
Oh My Love.

Skirts & Dresses
for First Time Sewers

Patterns, tutorials, tips, and advice

Christine Haynes

CONTENTS

Introduction 6

How to use this book 8

Chapter 1
The basics 12

Basic tools 14
Basic techniques 18
Choosing a size 28
Pattern layouts 30

Chapter 2
The projects 34

The A-line skirt 36
The tiered maxi skirt 42
The tunic dress 48
The smocked sundress 54
The baby doll dress 60
The upcycled T-shirt dress 66
The sleeveless sheath dress 72
The circle skirt 78
The slip dress 84
The wrap dress 90
The shift dress 96
The pleated skirt 102
The pencil skirt 108
The upcycled men's
  shirt skirt 114
The wrap skirt 120

Chapter 3
Trims and embellishments   **126**

Patch pockets   128
Shaped pockets   129
Appliqué   130
Lace and rickrack   131
Basic embroidery stitches   132

Chapter 4
Resources   **134**

Useful websites   136
Glossary   138
Contributor index   140

Index   **142**
Acknowledgments   **144**

INTRODUCTION

Learning to sew your own clothing is a wonderfully empowering feeling. Think about it—you are in charge. The idea that a skill like sewing is a craft of our old-fashioned past couldn't be more wrong. What is more modern than being in complete control of how your clothing looks, feels, and fits? Sewing always shows up at that moment in the movie when the leading lady takes charge of her life and makes something for herself to wear, then goes out into the world feeling fabulous and wins over the love she's after. Yes, this too can be you.

Sewing for yourself opens the door to understanding your body, the architecture of garments, textile design, and color—not to mention the business and politics of manufacturing. It can be the gateway to broadening your horizons and connecting with others interested in the same thing around the world. It sounds corny, but it can truly be a path to new and meaningful friendships and understanding. In addition to sewing for yourself, venturing down this path of learning will enable you to share this love and skill with others, both by making things for them, and by teaching what you know to those around you.

This book is designed to get you excited about two staples in your closet: skirts and dresses. Included are all the classic shapes that never go out of style, plus a few fun additions to get your creative juices flowing. Each design includes variations that suggest how to customize and change the original—but don't stop there. Let these act as jumping-off points to infuse each garment with your own personality and style.

As I say to all my students, don't be afraid to fail. Mistakes will happen whenever you learn something new. But keep at it; be fearless—before you know it you'll be getting compliments on your new handmade wardrobe!

Christine Haynes

HOW TO USE THIS BOOK

THE PROJECTS

Each project opens with two pages of images and text to introduce you to the style of that specific skirt or dress (see A). The images are not of the finished pattern included in the book, rather they are included for inspirational purposes—to show you many different ways to wear, style, change, and conceptualize your garment. The text helps to explain the style—how best to wear it, what body style it's best for, and what fabrics are ideal for the garment.

Following the opening pages is an illustration with the main view included in the patterns (see B), along with the supplies you will need, a list of the pattern pieces, steps for completing the project, and helpful tips to consider along the way. At the end of the steps are other styles to consider to customize your project and infuse the shape with your personal style (see C). To assist with personalizing your pieces, see Chapter 3 for tutorials on embellishments and trims.

THE PDF PATTERNS

All the patterns included in the book are formatted as PDF downloads. What this means is that the patterns I designed were sliced and diced and broken up to fit onto regular-sized paper so you can print them at home or at a local copy center. Each project has a QR code that you can scan with your smart device, but there is also a URL link for each pattern, so you can access them quickly on the Internet. Each page of the PDF files has a rectangle on it, with lines and shapes inside of it. The white space outside of the rectangle is the margin, to ensure that none of the actual pattern gets cut away off the edges of the paper during the printing process.

After downloading the pattern, do a test print. Each pattern file has one page with "test squares" on it. These squares need to be a specific size when printed, or else the pattern shape will be too large or too small, depending on how the printer is handling the pages. Print the test page first and measure the squares to make sure they are the correct size. If not, check the printing settings on your PDF reader software and make sure they are set to print at 100 percent without any automatic sizing or scaling.

Once the test square is right, and you have printed the pattern pages, it is time to assemble them! This can take a bit of time, but the great thing about having a reprintable pattern is that if you mess anything up, you can print it again! Another benefit of a PDF pattern is if you want to make it in a different size for a friend. There's no need to buy another pattern because you already cut yours out—simply print and assemble one in a different size. Easy!

When it comes to assembling, I like to trim the bottom and right sides of each page. This way all you need to do is line up the right and bottom sides of trimmed pages with the left and top edges of the consecutive pages. The lines and markings should all line up to form one big sheet of pattern pieces.

Please know that while the patterns are perfectly drafted, there is always some room for variance when using a home printer and the taped PDF method of pattern assembly. Slight shifts can occur and not everything will line up perfectly all the time. Do your best and reprint when necessary.

A

Information on the dress style and choosing your fabrics

B

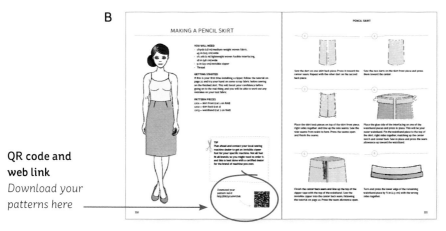

QR code and web link

Download your patterns here

C

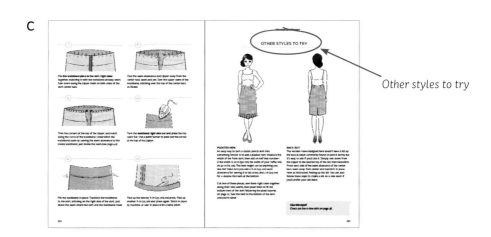

Other styles to try

CUTTING OUT YOUR PATTERNS AND FABRIC

Once you have your fabric (prewashed of course!), have assembled your printed pattern, and taken your body measurements to find your size (see page 28), it's time to cut out the pattern and pin it to your fabric.

Using paper scissors, follow the line for your size, cutting just outside the line. You don't want any extra paper left behind, but you do still want to be able to see the line marking out the pattern in your size.

Each project has a diagram showing how the pattern pieces will fit on the fabric (see pages 30–33). These are simply guidelines and if you want to do your own thing, that's fine by me! However, there are a few key factors to consider.

All the pattern pieces feature either a double-ended arrow line, or a bracket line with arrow ends pointing to one side of the pattern piece. The two-sided arrow line is the grainline (3). This line needs to be kept parallel with the lengthwise grain of the fabric (which runs parallel to the selvage edges) and pointing to the cut ends. This is hugely important; a garment's design takes into account the little bit of stretch built into a fabric from selvage to selvage, so placing a pattern piece in another direction will greatly affect fit and drape.

The bracket line with arrow ends points to a side of the pattern that needs to be placed on the fold of the fabric (4). You therefore cut out two sides of the same piece at once, such as a dress front. This not only halves the cutting time, but also ensures symmetry, and fabric is easier to cut when folded.

The pattern pieces used in some of the projects are too large to fit onto 45 in (115 cm)-wide fabrics and will only fit on 60 in (150 cm)-wide fabrics. These are noted at the start of a project, so make sure you read the material lists carefully!

Pin all the pattern pieces to the fabric, keeping them on the fold or the grainline, as required. Use fabric scissors to cut as close to the paper as possible, without actually cutting it. You want the fabric to be the exact same size as the pattern piece, so be sure not to cut under the pattern piece, or too far around it. From there, follow the steps of the project and you're set!

All of the patterns include seam allowances of ⅝ in (1.5 cm), unless otherwise indicated in the project's instructions. Places where you will find alternate seam allowances will be on small areas like tie belts, necklines, and straps. Make sure to read the instructions carefully to sew at the correct seam allowance for the step you are sewing! But if they don't specify otherwise, then it is a ⅝-in (1.5-cm) seam allowance.

1. Identify each pattern piece by looking for its number, then refer to the list supplied at the start of your project. For example, this layout shows the pattern pieces required for the baby doll dress, and the list on page 62 identifies 504 as the skirt back.

2. The selvage—the finished edges of the fabric, which run parallel to the grain.

3. The double-ended arrow line indicates the grainline. This must be kept parallel to the selvage.

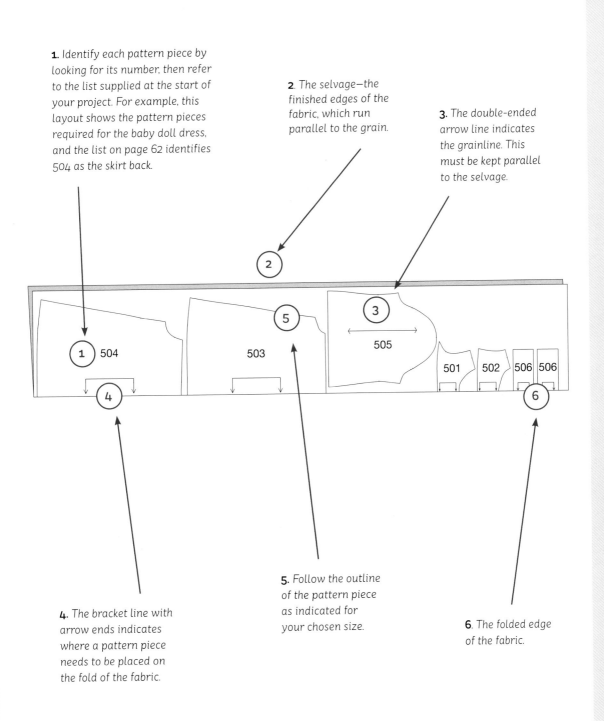

4. The bracket line with arrow ends indicates where a pattern piece needs to be placed on the fold of the fabric.

5. Follow the outline of the pattern piece as indicated for your chosen size.

6. The folded edge of the fabric.

CHAPTER 1
THE BASICS

Basic tools   **14**

Basic techniques   **18**

Simple darts   18
Contour darts   19
Gathering   20
Pleats   21
Inserting an invisible zipper   22
Seam finishing   24
Hand sewing   25
Making your own bias tape   26

Choosing a size   **28**

Pattern layouts   **30**

Opposite: Daisy jacquard dress by Dunnes Stores.

BASIC TOOLS

Every sewer needs a handful of tools to make the job easier. Think of it like a kitchen: It is hard to blend something without a blender. The same is true with your sewing supplies—it will be tricky to do certain things without the right tool for the job. There are endless items on the market, but shown on these pages are the basics that everyone should have at their disposal. Once you've outgrown these, it's time to branch out into other, more specialized, equipment.

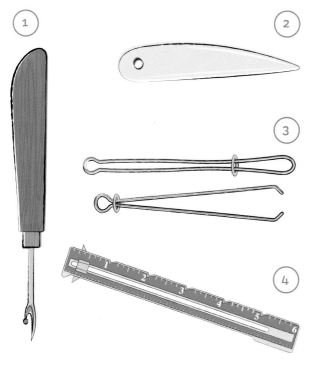

8-inch scissors might feel too big. This is a perfect moment for a smaller version of the large pair, so you don't cut something you didn't mean to.

Paper scissors
Keep an inexpensive pair of scissors in your studio for cutting paper patterns, opening boxes, and so on. This will preserve your nice pair much longer.

SEAM RIPPER (1)
The reality is, you will make a mistake, although there are many reasons to use a seam ripper other than just to undo something you messed up. A basting (temporary) stitch is meant to be a placeholder while you sew the real stitch. After it's sewn, the basting stitch needs to be removed—a perfect task for your seam ripper. But of course, you will also need it for undoing mistakes too!

PINS
Depending on the fabric you are using, you will need a variety of pins on hand. The pins I use most and suggest getting—if you were to get just one type—are glass-head pins. The glass ball prevents them from being melted by the heat of an iron, and also helps you see the pins while sewing, so you can pull them out before stitching over them. There are different pins available for silk, knits, or other specialty fabrics, but if you are working with lightweight to medium-weight woven fabrics, the basic glass-head pin will suit most of your needs.

RULER
You will measure many things along the way while sewing, and the best item for that is a clear ruler, around 2 in (5 cm) wide and 18 in (45 cm) long. Being able to see the fabric through the plastic is a critical element, so if you only have an opaque ruler, I suggest investing in a clear one that lets you line

SCISSORS
Other than your sewing machine, the most important tool in your kit is a pair of scissors. Keep multiple pairs for different tasks so you don't end up dulling your nice shears doing something like cutting paper. There are three main types you should consider investing in.

8-inch dressmaker's shears
I prefer an all-metal pair that can be sharpened. Use these only for cutting fabric, ribbon, and similar fibers, and store them where they won't get banged around.

5-inch scissors
Sometimes you will need to cut small amounts of fabric while trimming the inside of a project, and your

things up with the grid on the ruler when making marks or cutting your fabric.

TAPE MEASURE

While a ruler is perfect for measuring flat things, your body isn't exactly flat, and you will need the flexibility of a tape measure for taking body measurements. Find one that is made of fiberglass, as it won't stretch, shrink, or warp with time.

POINT TURNER (2)

This does exactly as its name implies—makes a crisp point. Use the pointed end on any right angle, such as on a collar or pillow, and the rounded end to push out curved seams. The point isn't sharp, so you can poke out corners without cutting or tearing the fabric or threads.

BODKIN (3)

Many sewers get by for decades without a bodkin, but it really is a wonderful tool. It is basically a fancy pair of tweezers with a stopper on the end. Place something that needs to go into a casing—like elastic or a drawstring—clamp down the stopper, and feed it safely through the casing until you get to the other end. Voila!

SEAM GAUGE (4)

People always ask me what my favorite tool is, and the answer is always a 6-in (15-cm) seam gauge—a mini-ruler with a slide on it that marks the measurement you are using. It is perfect for tasks that your ruler is just too big for, such as marking buttonholes or folding up hems. I love the precision of being able to measure down to a very small amount.

CHALK PENCILS

The most precise tool for making marks on your fabric is a sharpened chalk pencil. I prefer pencils that are water soluble. Non-water-soluble is fine too—just be careful to test the chalk on the fabric before marking on the right side of your fabric.

HAND-SEWING NEEDLES

You will have many opportunities to stitch something by hand, so you will need some hand-sewing needles around to get the job done. There are hundreds of types

on the market, but I would suggest getting a pack of sharps, milliner's needles, and crewel needles—each one gets larger and longer, so you can use them for a multitude of projects.

THREAD

Like all raw materials in sewing, thread comes in a range of fiber contents, and the choice of which to use can be somewhat subjective. The main threads you will encounter are 100 percent polyester, 100 percent cotton, and cotton-wrapped polyester, which is just as it sounds—a core of cotton wrapped with an outer layer of polyester. Silk thread, rayon thread, and a lot of other kinds are out there too. Generally speaking, it is a good idea to pair natural fibers like cotton and linen fabrics with cotton thread, and to use polyester thread with synthetic fabrics.

SEWING-MACHINE NEEDLES

Pairing the weight of your needle with the weight of your fabric is very important. If you use a needle that is too heavy and thick with a lightweight fabric, it will leave behind a hole that is far too large; if you pair a thin, lightweight needle with a heavy fabric, there is a chance it will break in half. Needles come in many types and sizes, so when purchasing one, keep in mind both the weight and the type of fabric so the combination will result in a well-sewn seam. Lightweight and medium-weight woven fabrics are best sewn with size 70/11 or 80/12 Microtex Sharps needles respectively. Lightweight and medium-weight knit fabrics require a ball-point needle of the same size.

PRESSING TOOLS

Apart from basic pressing tools, like an iron and ironing board, a pressing (tailor's) ham will also be helpful. This fills the space where your body will be when pressing sections of the garments that are no longer flat after sewing, such as a shoulder or bust dart.

SEWING MACHINE

Clearly, the sewing machine is not an item to overlook when thinking about sewing! It will be your number one tool and, if well chosen and cared for, it will become a good friend on your sewing journey. When buying a machine, think of it like a car or some other high-tech tool—you always want to get the best you can afford, but having one is always better than not having one.

The best suggestion I can make is to find one with as many metal moving parts as possible, as metal will wear and age better than plastic moving parts. The machine will also be more stable while sewing, and the mechanisms will be more precise. But again, any machine is better than no machine, so do the best that you can.

Know that not all sewing machines have all the same buttons and knobs, nor will they all be in the same place, so I highly recommend consulting the instruction manual to find out how to use your specific machine. Most sewing machines, though, will have the following key items:

Hand wheel (1)
Attached to the belt inside the machine that makes everything move. Only turn this dial toward you; if turned away from you, the threads will become tangled.

Foot pedal (2)
This foot-operated pedal is used to power the machine.

Stitch width (3)
This dial controls how wide the threads move from side to side. When set to zero, the thread stays straight, resulting in a straight stitch.

Stitch length (4)
A stitch can be as long or short as you like, although the common all-purpose length is 2.5 mm. The higher this dial is turned up, the longer the stitch will be.

Spool pin (5) and bobbin (6)
Two spools of thread form each stitch—your actual spool of thread, which lives on the spool pin, and the bobbin, housed internally, beneath the foot plate. Your manual will explain how to load and insert your bobbin.

Reverse button (7)
When starting and ending a stitch, you will do a backstitch, which requires you to sew in reverse. This button will allow you to move backward.

Stitch selection (8)
Most machines come with a number of stitches, from utilitarian to fancy. This knob will let you switch from stitch to stitch, depending on your sewing needs.

Presser foot (9)
Most machines comes with a handful of basic presser feet, and of course there are tons of optional feet that you can buy that will do everything under the sun. The main feet you will want for basic sewing—and to make all the projects in this book—are the all-purpose foot for everyday sewing, the regular zipper foot, the invisible zipper foot, and the buttonhole foot. My favorite specialty feet are the blind hem foot and the ¼-in (0.7-cm) seam foot—both entirely optional.

Foot plate and feed dogs (10)
There are a couple of important items under the presser foot. The foot plate is the metal piece with marks and measurements on it. This is where you set your fabric when sewing. Your fabric should be alongside the measurement of the seam allowance for the project you are sewing. In the middle of the foot plate are metal teeth poking up. These are the feed dogs and it's their job to pull the fabric through the machine as it sews.

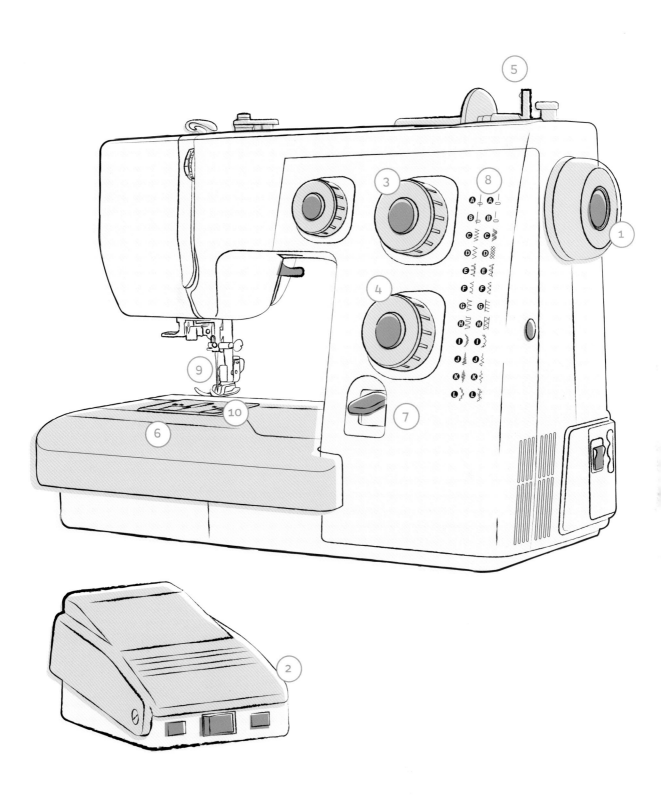

BASIC TECHNIQUES

There are entire encyclopedias dedicated to sewing techniques, but for the purpose of making the garments in this book we are going to focus on learning some of the building blocks so you can move onto any of the projects that follow with confidence.

SIMPLE DARTS

A dart sounds fancy, but it is simply a fold in the fabric that you sew in place to shape the fabric around your curves. It's as easy as that! You will mark your darts after you have cut your pattern piece from the fabric, but before you've unpinned the paper pattern. Make sure the wrong side of the fabric is facing up, so you aren't making marks on the right side.

1

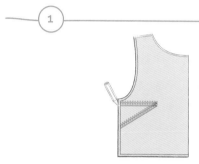

Mark the ends of a dart at the side seam with chalk pencil. Insert a pin into the apex of the dart and peel back the pattern paper. Mark the spot where the pin was inserted with a dot.

2

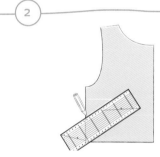

Draw a line from the apex dot to the other ends of the dart. These are the dart legs.

3

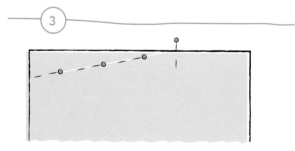

Insert a pin at the end of each dart leg and at the apex. Fold the dart, right sides of the fabric together, and line up the pins at the dart legs. Pin along the leg of the dart facing you, keeping the line on the underside even with the leg on top.

4

Insert the fabric into your machine, starting at the fabric edge. Make a backstitch by sewing forward a few stitches, then reversing back to the start, then sew along the line to the dart apex. About 1 in (2.5 cm) before the apex, stop and reduce the stitch length to 1.0 mm, then continue. Don't backstitch at the apex—sew right off the edge of the fabric (the stitches will stay nice and tight).

Clip the threads on each end and press the dart according to the project instructions. A pressing (tailor's) ham placed under the dart will help take the place of the curve that the dart was shaped for, as the fabric will no longer want to lay flat.

CONTOUR DARTS

A contour dart can look intimidating, but it simply involves sewing two regular darts with the widest part of the darts facing each other. These are most commonly used at the waist for shaping around the curves in the middle of the body. As with a basic dart, your pattern piece should already be cut from fabric, and marking should be done on the wrong side of the fabric.

1

Insert a pin at one dart apex and at the center point where the darts meet. Repeat by inserting a pin at the opposite dart apex. Peel back the pattern piece carefully and mark these spots with a dot, using a chalk pencil.

2

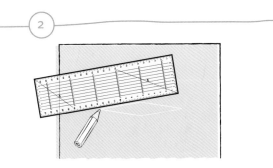

Remove the pattern paper and draw a line connecting one apex with the center point. Repeat with the other side of the dart. Your shape should look something like a diamond.

3

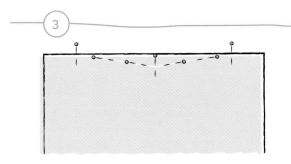

Just as you would with a basic dart, fold the fabric, right sides together, and insert a pin at each apex. Insert another pin at the center point, where the darts meet. Make sure the pin goes through the spot marked on each side. Pin along each dart leg to the apex, keeping in line with the underside markings.

4

Insert your fabric into your sewing machine with the needle inserted at the center point where the darts meet. Sew a backstitch and sew along the line to the apex. When you are 1 in (2.5 cm) away from the end of the dart leg, stop and reduce the stitch length to 1.0 mm. Sew along the rest of the dart and off the fabric. Repeat this whole step on the other side of the dart, remembering to turn your stitch length back to a regular setting before starting the other side.

5

Clip the extra threads and make a snip in the fabric at the center point of the dart, where the two darts meet. Press the darts with a pressing ham underneath.

GATHERING

The concept of gathering is quite simple—you take a piece of fabric that is wider than another piece of fabric, and gather it to fit using long stitches (basting stitches). It is pretty easy, and you will see it on many projects in this book, so it's a great thing to get familiar with!

Place the piece to be gathered into the machine, with the top edge on the ⅜-in (1-cm) seam allowance. Turn your stitch length up to 4.0 or 5.0 mm. Sew a straight stitch across the edge to be gathered, but avoid backstitching at the start and end of it (we want these threads to move and not be locked in place). This is your basting stitch. Leave long thread ends on either side of the stitch. These will be used later to gather the stitches.

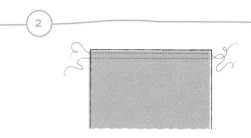

Repeat Step 1, but this time sew basting stitches along the ¾-in (2-cm) seam allowance. Again, make sure to leave long threads at the start and finish of your row.

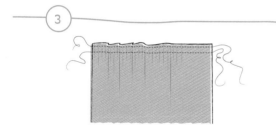

Place the piece to be gathered and the piece it is being sewn to, right sides together. Pin in place at each end and at the center point. Lay these down, with the basted piece on the top layer facing you.

Holding onto the bobbin threads of your basting stitches, scoot the fabric along the threads between one end and the center until the distance of the larger piece matches the smaller piece underneath. Even out the gathering and pin in place. Repeat on the other half of the piece.

Insert the whole piece into the sewing machine with the gathered side up and sew a regular straight stitch with a ⅝-in (1.5-cm) seam allowance, which should place your stitching right in the middle of your two previous rows of stitches.

Remove the basting stitches and press the seam according to the project instructions. The basting stitches should pull right out since they are long and loose, but if not, seek assistance from your seam ripper.

PLEATS

Making pleats is much like gathering—reducing a larger fabric to fit a smaller fabric. The only difference is that instead of gathering the fabric up with basting stitches, the fabric is folded to form equal folds, which are the pleats. There are many styles of pleat, but for the purposes of this book, we are just going to look at the classic knife pleat.

①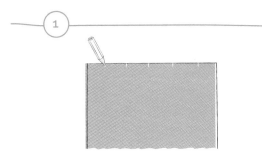

Using the pattern piece as your guide, transfer the pleat marks from the paper to the fabric. These marks are to be made on the right side of the fabric, so I recommend using a marking tool that is water soluble and making your marks light so they will come out with ease.

②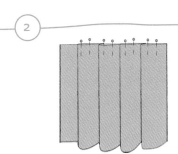

Insert pins into these marks. Fold the fabric along the fold lines and line up the pins. Pin all the layers together so the pleat is pinned in place. Repeat with all of the pleats until they are folded all along the required seam.

③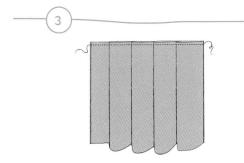

Stitch the pleats in place, sewing with a slightly smaller seam allowance than the project calls for, so your stitches will be hidden on the finished garment.

④

Press the pleats, either just at the top for a soft pleat, or all the way to the hem for a crisp pleat. Continue with the project's instructions to finish the garment.

INSERTING AN INVISIBLE ZIPPER

The idea of inserting a zipper can frighten a lot of new sewers, but don't be afraid—this isn't nearly as hard as you think! I think a poorly sewn regular zipper screams "home made," and they can be tricky to sew perfectly. I prefer an invisible zipper, since there is no exterior stitching showing, making your sewing visible only on the inside of the garment. The finish is much more professional too, since the zipper is concealed in a seam with only the top pull showing. A note of caution: You can only insert this type of zipper correctly with an invisible zipper foot. This doesn't usually come with sewing machines, so call the local dealer for your sewing machine brand to get an invisible zipper foot—sometimes also called a concealed zipper foot.

Lay your invisible zipper down on your ironing board, with the wrong side up. This is the side with the teeth and not the pull. Open the zipper and press the teeth of the zipper with an iron. The teeth should start curled like the letter "C" toward the zipper tape, and end like the letter "L" after pressing. Repeat on the other side of the zipper.

Lay the zipper on the left side of the fabric, right sides together. The zipper teeth should be at the seam allowance for the project, and the top of the zipper in position based on the project instructions. Typically the seam allowance is ⅝ in (1.5 cm) and the top is either ⅝ in (1.5 cm) from the fabric, or flush, depending on how the rest of the seam is finished. Pin in place.

The seam that the zipper is going into should not be sewn yet, but you will want to finish the edges of the seam before inserting the zipper. Take a moment and finish the seam in your desired method—with a zigzag stitch, serger machine, or pinking shears (see page 24, Seam Finishing).

With the invisible zipper foot on your machine, insert the teeth into the left channel on the foot. The right edge of the fabric should be in line with your seam allowance. Sew a backstitch. Keep the teeth in the channel and sew to the bottom of the zipper. Backstitch as close as you can to the end of the teeth where the pull is.

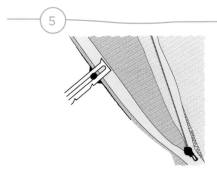

5

Flip the zipper twice, ending right side down on the right side of the other piece of fabric. Make sure you position it in the exact same spot as you did on the first side. If it is lower or higher, the other elements of the seam will not line up.

6

Insert the fabric into the sewing machine, this time placing the teeth into the right side of the zipper foot. This can be awkward as the excess fabric will now be on the right of the foot instead of its usual spot on the left of the foot. Keep in line with your seam allowance on the left of the foot and sew all the way down to the bottom of the zipper.

Not all machines will have seam allowance guidelines to the left of the presser foot. If yours doesn't, with your needle set to a straight stitch, simply measure from the needle to the left, and mark your seam allowance with a piece of tape or a sticky note. You will need the correct measurement to sew the zipper at the right place.

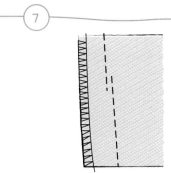

7

Change from an invisible zipper foot to a regular zipper foot. Pin the fabric in place from the end of the zipper to the end of the seam. Sew as close as you can to the end of the stitching, then sew all the way to the end of the seam, keeping on your seam allowance for the project you are working on.

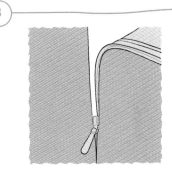

8

Press the seam on the right side and press the seam allowance open on the wrong side. You're done!

SEAM FINISHING

Cut fabric will fray and eventually weaken the seams you've spent so much time sewing. No one wants their clothes to pop while wearing them, so it's worth taking a little time during construction to finish the seams! Many patterns will not instruct you as to how and when you should do this; it is just implied. But for the projects in this book, I have made a point of telling you when it's best to take care of this important step. There are many ways to finish a seam, but the easiest is a zigzag stitch finish.

1

Set your sewing machine to a zigzag stitch with a medium length and width. Insert your fabric into the machine and sew just on the inside of your fabric's raw edge. There is no need to backstitch, as this is an interior stitch rather than a construction stitch.

2

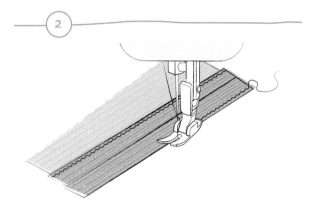

Sew along the edge of your fabric until you reach the end. Repeat on the other side of your seam.

3

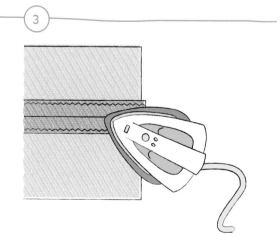

Press the seam according to the project instructions.

HAND SEWING

There are a few basic hand-sewing techniques that will prove helpful along the way. These two are my favorite and most used.

HEM STITCH

If you are looking for an invisible finish on the hem of any garment, this stitch can be done by hand instead of stitching with a machine.

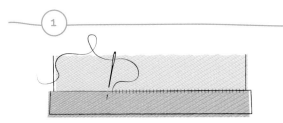

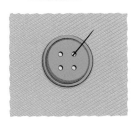

Insert your threaded needle into the top fold of the hem. Just above the hem, catch a tiny bit of the fabric on the finished part of the garment. Only sew through a bit, as you will see it on the right side of the hem.

Repeat by sewing through the fold of the hem, about 1 in (2.5 cm) from the previous stitch. Keep your stitches tiny and equally spaced so they look clean on the right side. Keep going until you've made it all the way around the hem.

SEWING ON A BUTTON

No matter where your sewing career ends up going, this is one of those things that everyone needs to know!

Mark where you want to sew your button. Thread your needle and pass it from the underside of your fabric through to the right side, through one of the holes in the button. Now insert the needle back through an adjacent hole to complete one stitch.

Continue passing the needle through the holes of the button and back through the fabric. Repeat this until the button is secure.

To finish, thread the needle through the underside of the fabric, leave a loop, and pass the needle through the loop to form a knot. Repeat and then cut off the excess thread.

MAKING YOUR OWN BIAS TAPE

Bias tape, or bias binding, is not actually tape, but rather strips of fabric cut on the bias. The bias of a fabric occurs at a 45-degree angle across its threads, where the stretch is greatest on woven fabrics. Because of this stretch, bias tape can travel effortlessly around curves, so is used on necklines, armholes, and hems; you could even press bias tape into a perfectly round circle if you wanted to. It is an easy way to finish edges, and can add a pop of color if used as an accent.

Many of this book's projects rely on double-fold bias tape for casings, neckline finishing, and waistband ties, so if you want to make your own, follow this easy tutorial. You can always buy pre-made bias tape, but it's so rewarding to have homemade bias binding in a fun print!

---

(1)

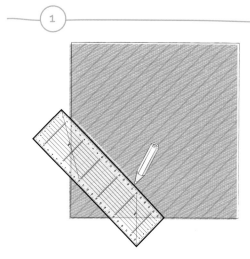

Draw a 45-degree angled line across the fabric. To find the angle, use a ruler with angles marked on it. Simply place the 45-degree angle mark along the selvage so the ruler goes into the fabric at that angle. If your ruler doesn't have that mark on it, fold the fabric back to create a 45-degree fold to use as your guide. Draw lines 2 in (5 cm) apart, which will be the starting width of your double-fold bias tape.

---

(2)

Cut along the lines you drew. Cut as many strips as you will need for the project you are making. Not sure how much you'll need? Use your tape measure to get a rough measurement, then make a little more than that because you will lose some in the joining of the strips. Trim the ends of the strips so they are at a 90-degree angle to the strips.

---

(3)

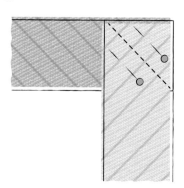

Place the strips right sides together, forming a right angle at the corner. Pin in place and draw a line from the top left corner to the lower right corner. This is your sewing line. Make sure the top and right sides of the two strips are perfectly in line.

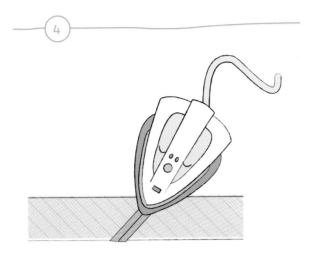

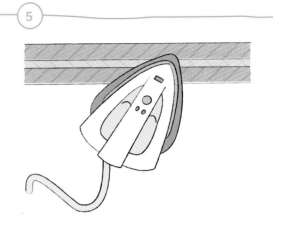

Sew along the line you drew in Step 3, being sure to backstitch at the beginning and end of the stitch. Trim the seam allowance down to ¼ in (0.7 cm), then press it open.

To create the double fold, first fold the strip in half, wrong sides together, lining up the top edges and press. Open the fold up and fold one half into the central fold, wrong sides together, and press. Repeat by folding the other side into the center and press. Be careful not to press over the central fold while folding in the two sides. You should have three folds creating four equal parts on the strip.

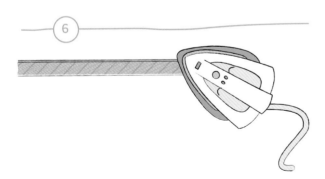

Fold the whole tape closed, fitting the folds to the inside and being very careful to line up the top edges so the top and bottom layers of the bias tape are exactly the same size. Now it's ready to be sewn into your project!

CHOOSING A SIZE

The garments in this book are either loose or semifitted. This is deliberate because when you are starting to sew for yourself, the first concern should not be fit; it should be about sewing straight, learning how to press folds, and other basic elements. Though of course, no one wants their dresses to be overly large or, worse, too small!

The best thing to do is to check the measurement chart shown opposite in relation to your own body measurements. But it is also important to keep in mind the style of the garment and how much ease might be built into the design based on the shape.

What is ease you ask? Ease is the distance between your body and the garment. Fitted dresses typically have 2 in (5 cm) or less ease so they are fitted snugly around the body. Loose garments, like the shift dress project on page 96, are meant to hang and flow around the body with a much greater amount of ease. This has all been accounted for in the sizing of the patterns, but it may be a comfort to know that if you were to be a bit too large, the dress would be entirely wearable as it's meant to be free flowing.

To properly measure your body, it's best to get into your undergarments. You will need the bust support of your bra, so do not take your measurements in the nude. Grab a tape measure and stand in front of a full-length mirror. For the bust measurement, hold the tape measure around the fullest part of your bust. Make sure the tape measure is level across your back and that the tape is pulled snug.

For the waist, bend to the side and find where your body naturally creases around the belly button. This is your natural waist. Take the tape measure and wrap it around your body at this point. Keep it snug but make sure you are not holding your breath or looking down. Both will affect the measurement.

For your hip, measure down 9 in (23 cm) from the waist, or at the fullest part of your hip across your backside. This again should be measured with a snugly pulled tape measure. Mark down those measurements and compare them to the ones included in the size chart to find the best size for you.

Sometimes pattern adjustments need to be made, and this is entirely common—it is nearly impossible for any one pattern to fit all the bodies of the world. Making a test garment, or a muslin, is always a good habit to get into. This can be done in muslin fabric, or any inexpensive fabric of your choice, just as long as it is similar in weight and content to the final fabric. For pattern adjustments, such as a full bust adjustment or blending sizes, simply consult your favorite sewing blogs for tutorials, including mine! (See page 136.)

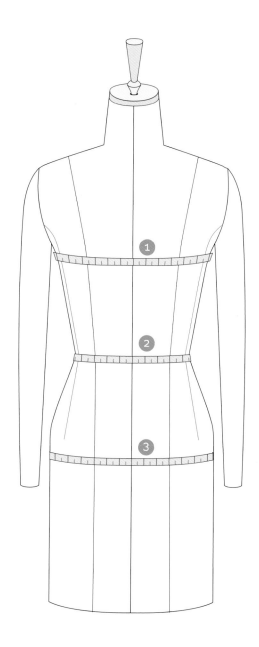

	Inches	SIZE 1	SIZE 2	SIZE 3	SIZE 4	SIZE 5	Own measurements
①	Bust	31–32	33–34½	36–37½	39–41	43–45	
②	Waist	23–24	25–26½	28–29½	31–33	35–37	
③	Hip	33–34	35–36½	38–39½	41–43	45–47	
	Centimeters						
①	Bust	79–81	84–88	91.5–95	99–114	109–114	
②	Waist	58.5–61	63.5–66	71–73.5	78.5–84	89–94	
③	Hip	84–86	89–93	96.5–100	104–109	114–119	

PATTERN LAYOUTS

These are my suggestions for the most efficient way of laying out your pattern pieces for each of the projects included in the book. (No pattern pieces are required for the upcycled projects.)

A-line skirt (all sizes) / 45 in (115 cm)-wide fabric

A-line skirt (all sizes) / 18 in (46 cm)-wide interfacing

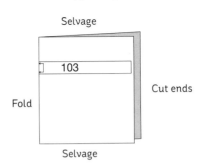

Baby doll dress (all sizes) / 45 in (115 cm)-wide fabric

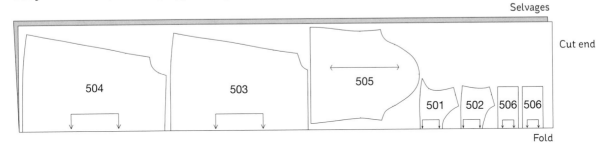

Pencil skirt (all sizes) / 45 in (115 cm)-wide fabric

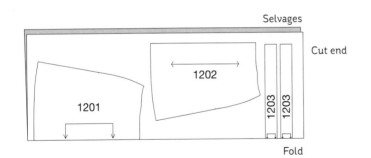

Pencil skirt (all sizes) / 18 in (46 cm)-wide interfacing

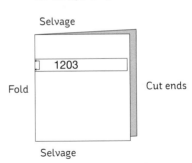

Circle skirt (all sizes) / 60 in (150 cm)-wide fabric

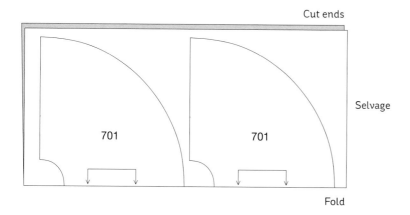

Tiered maxi skirt (all sizes) / 60 in (150 cm)-wide fabric

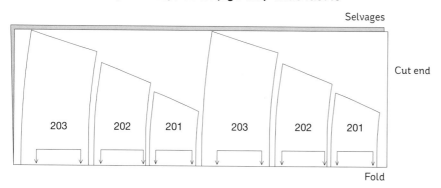

Pleated skirt (all sizes) / 60 in (150 cm)-wide fabric

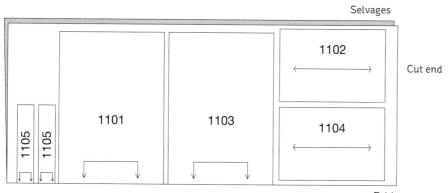

Smocked sundress (all sizes) / 45 in (115 cm)-wide fabric

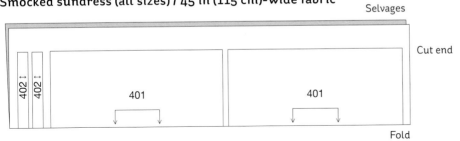

Selvages

Cut end

402 ↕

402 ↕

401

401

Fold

Wrap skirt (all sizes) / 45 in (115 cm)-wide fabric

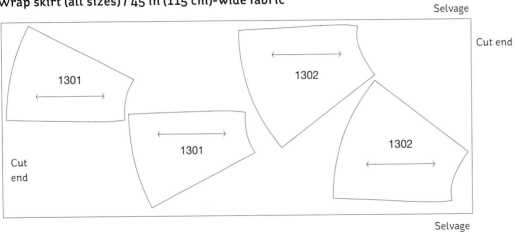

Selvage

Cut end

1301

1302

1301

1302

Cut
end

Selvage

Wrap dress (all sizes) / 45 in (115 cm)-wide fabric

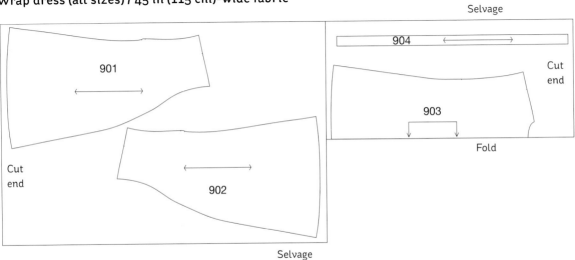

Selvage

901

904

Cut
end

903

902

Cut
end

Fold

Selvage

Sleeveless sheath dress (all sizes) / 45 in (115 cm)-wide fabric

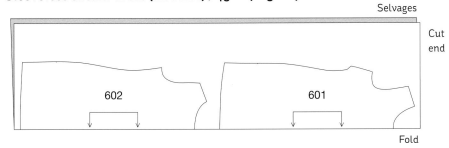

Shift dress (all sizes) / 45 in (115 cm)-wide fabric

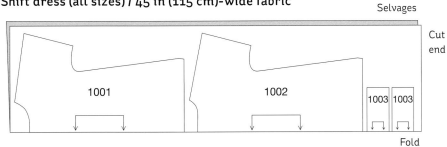

Slip dress (all sizes) / 45 in (115 cm)-wide fabric

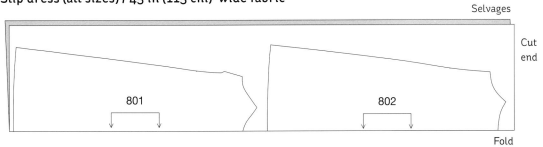

Tunic dress (all sizes) / 45 in (115 cm)-wide fabric

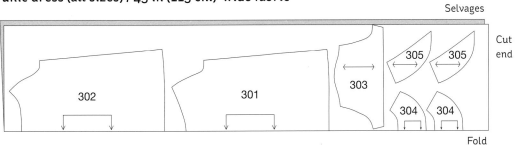

CHAPTER 2
THE PROJECTS

The A-line skirt	36
The tiered maxi skirt	42
The tunic dress	48
The smocked sundress	54
The baby doll dress	60
The upcycled T-shirt dress	66
The sleeveless sheath dress	72
The circle skirt	78
The slip dress	84
The wrap dress	90
The shift dress	96
The pleated skirt	102
The pencil skirt	108
The upcycled men's shirt skirt	114
The wrap skirt	120

Opposite: Terry jersey dress by Nancy Dee Brooke.

THE A-LINE SKIRT

When you think of a timeless skirt that suits nearly every body type and every social situation, the A-line skirt is likely to be the first thing to come to mind. A favorite through the ages, from Jackie O to Carrie Bradshaw, every chic woman should have a few A-line skirts in her repertoire.

This skirt is easy to dress up or down, depending on your personal style. It's a great all-season choice—it looks good in the summer paired with strappy sandals, and in winter with tights and boots. This skirt is always a classic choice.

Key characteristics
The shape of an A-line skirt is just as it sounds—it is shaped a bit like the letter A, getting wider as it follows along the curve of your hip to the hem with a slight flare.

Who does it suit?
The A shape of the skirt is best on ladies who have a smaller waist than hip measurement, rather than the other way around. This skirt is fitted at the body's natural waist, so be watchful if you are short waisted as it might feel a bit high on the body.

Suitable fabrics
Since this skirt has some structure to it, it is best made up in a fabric with some body, so avoid anything too flowy or drapey, and stick to medium-weight woven fabrics such as cotton, linen, or lightweight corduroy and wool. Since there are minimal seams, this is a great opportunity to feature a favorite print. Or whip one up in a solid color for the ultimate wardrobe staple.

Styling tips
The A-line skirt is so classic, it is a blank canvas waiting to be styled by you. It works just as well worn with a pussy-bow blouse and pumps for the office as it does teamed with a favorite concert T-shirt and boots when going out with friends.

Opposite: Black skirt by La Redoute (l); Beige stretch satin skirt by La Redoute (r). **Above:** Vintage leather skirt, styled by Emily Lane (t); Cotton print prom skirt by M&Co (b).

MAKING AN A-LINE SKIRT

YOU WILL NEED

- 1⅝ yds (1.5 m) of medium-weight woven fabric, 45 in (115 cm) wide
- 1⅛ yds (1 m) of lightweight woven fusible interfacing, 18 in (46 cm) wide
- 9-in (23-cm) invisible zipper
- Thread

GETTING STARTED

As with any project, begin by taking accurate body measurements and select the size you want to make by referencing the measurement chart on page 29. This project relies on your natural waist and hip measurements. Once you've selected your size and fabric, prewash your fabric according to the manufacturer's instructions and press flat. Cut out all necessary pieces and follow along to make your next favorite garment!

PATTERN PIECES

101 = skirt front (cut 1 on fold)
102 = skirt back (cut 2)
103 = waistband (cut 2 fabric, cut 1 interfacing)

TIP

Making a muslin, or practice version, of any garment can be a huge help with solving any fitting issues before cutting into your "real" fabric. Once you've made pattern changes to custom-fit the item, you can move forward with confidence!

Download your pattern here:
http://bit.ly/1wkROrr

1 Sew the darts on the skirt front piece and press toward the center. Sew the darts on the skirt back pieces in the same way and press toward the center back. For help in sewing darts, refer to page 18.

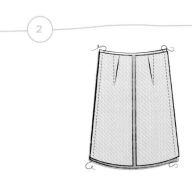

2 Place the skirt back pieces on top of the skirt front piece, right sides together. Sew the side seams from waist to hem. Press the seams open and finish the seams.

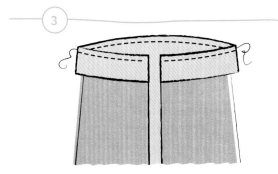

3 Place the glue side of the interfacing on one of the waistband pieces and press in place. This will be your outer waistband. Pin this piece to the top of the skirt, right sides together, matching up the center notch and center back. Sew in place, open the waistband, and press the seam allowance up toward the waistband.

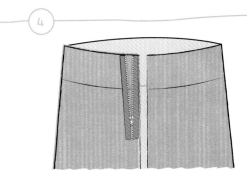

4 Finish the center back seam and line up the top of the zipper tape with the top of the waistband. Sew the invisible zipper into the center back seam, following the instructions on page 22. Press the seam allowance open.

5 Turn and press the lower edge of the remaining waistband piece by ⅝ in (1.5 cm), with wrong sides together.

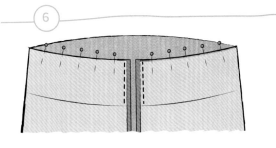

6 Pin this waistband piece to the skirt, right sides together, matching it with the waistband already sewn. Sew down along the zipper teeth on both sides of the skirt center back.

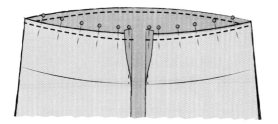

Fold the seam allowance and zipper away from the center back seam and pin. Sew the upper seam of the waistband, stitching over the top of the center back as folded. To reduce bulk and allow the curve seam to lay flat we will next cut some notches.

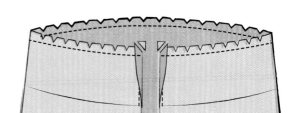

Cut small triangles into the seam allowance. Trim the corners at the top of the zipper. Understitch the waistband seam by sewing the seam allowance to the inside waistband, just inside the seam. This helps keep the waistband rolled to the inside of the skirt.

Turn the waistband right side out and press the top seam flat. Use a point turner to poke out the corners at the top of the zipper.

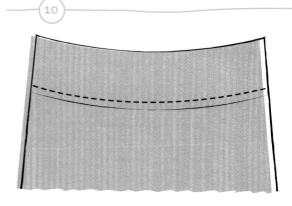

Pin the waistband in place. Topstitch the waistband to the skirt, stitching on the right side of the skirt, just above the seam where the skirt and the waistband meet.

Fold up the hem of the skirt ½ in (1.25 cm) and press. Fold another ½ in (1.25 cm) and press again. Stitch in place by machine, or sew in place with a hand stitch (see page 25).

OTHER STYLES TO TRY

CONTRAST TOPSTITCHING

Take inspiration from your jeans and try topstitching all the seams in a contrasting thread. Sew the side seams in Step 2, and then stitch down either side of the seam in a different color. Top off the stitching by sewing the waistband and hem with the same contrasting thread. Remember, though, if you're drawing attention to your seams, you want to take your time and sew them straight! You can also adjust the length of your skirt when cutting out your pattern pieces. Simply reduce by the same amount at the hem of both the front and back pieces.

CHANGE THE WAIST

Try making up the skirt in one fabric and the waistband in a contrasting fabric. This could be two prints, two solids, or one could be a print and the other a solid. Take inspiration from your favorite stores or catalogs and learn how to mix fabrics and prints!

Like this style?
Check out the pencil skirt on page 108.

THE TIERED MAXI SKIRT

Any garment that hits the floor is going to have some built-in drama, and the maxi skirt is no exception. But unlike a red-carpet gown, the maxi skirt can also be very casual and down to earth—it is a chameleon that can really change its tone and appearance depending on the fabric used and the accessories it's paired with.

Toss on a floral printed maxi skirt with strappy sandals and a favorite T-shirt and you're ready to walk the beach boardwalk; but slip on a black maxi skirt, change into heels, and put on a sequin tank and suddenly it's appropriate for a fancy party. That's the thing about a maxi skirt—it can really work in any situation!

Key characteristics
The maxi skirt by definition is long—usually floor length. Typically a fuller skirt, it drapes from the waist and over the hips in an A-line shape. It can be made of a single fabric, cut into tiers or panels, or feature a large bottom ruffle.

Who does it suit?
Despite the belief that only tall ladies can wear a maxi skirt, this is not true! Women of any height—and most shapes—can wear one. If you are fuller in the hip than the waist, wearing it on your hips might be more comfortable and flattering.

Suitable fabrics
Stick to lightweight to medium-weight woven fabrics with good drape, such as lawn, voile, rayon, silk, and cotton gauze. Hold up your fabric, gather it to simulate your waist, and study how it falls from that point. If it has stiff angles, it's not a good choice; if it hangs with a fluid drape it's ideal!

Styling tips
Since this skirt is full and demands a lot of real estate on your body, keep the top half simple. For a casual look, a classic white tank, T-shirt, or button-down with a hip-slung belt works well. For a fancier affair, a fitted cardigan or top and a simple clutch will keep it dressy but not too overdone.

Opposite: Cotton maxi skirt with lace appliqué hem by La Redoute.
Above: Red cotton maxi skirt by La Redoute (t); Vintage maxi skirt, styled by Jean Dotts (b).

MAKING A TIERED MAXI SKIRT

YOU WILL NEED

- 2⅓ yds (2.2 m) lightweight woven fabric, 60 in (150 cm) wide
- Elastic, ¾ in (2 cm) wide
- Thread

GETTING STARTED

Since this garment relies on hitting the floor, you might want to consider the length in relation to your height before cutting. Measure from the place you want to wear it on your body to the floor while wearing either flats or heels, and compare that to the finished length measurement on the pattern. From there you can adjust the length accordingly.

PATTERN PIECES

201 = top skirt tier (cut 2 on fold)
202 = middle skirt tier (cut 2 on fold)
203 = bottom skirt tier (cut 2 on fold)

TIP
Be sure to sew your skirt layers together at the ⅝-in (1.5-cm) seam allowance. That way each tier will line up when you go to sew the side seams together, and the fabric will also have a continuous seam around the body.

Download your pattern here:
http://bit.ly/1mNStAf

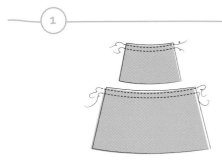

1 Sew basting stitches along the top edge of the middle and lower tiers of the skirt at the ⅜-in (1-cm) and ¾-in (2-cm) seam allowances.

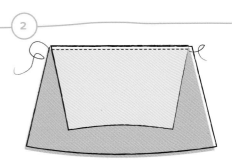

2 Place the lower edge of the top tier in line with the top edge of the middle tier, right sides together. Gather the middle tier to fit and stitch. Repeat with the other set of top and middle tiers. Remove the basting stitches. (See page 20 for tips on gathering fabric properly.)

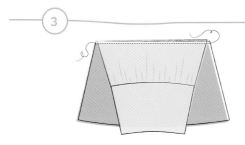

3 Place the lower edge of the middle tier in line with the top edge of the bottom tier, right sides together. Gather the lower tier to fit and stitch. Repeat with the other set of middle and bottom tiers. Remove the basting stitches.

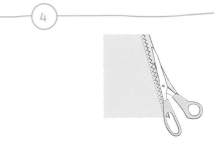

4 Finish all the seams sewn in Steps 2 and 3 with zigzag stitches at ⅜ in (1 cm) through both layers of the seam allowance. Trim away the extra fabric and press the seam allowances toward the waist.

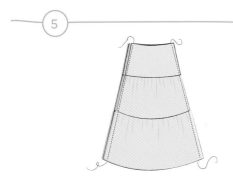

5 Place the skirt back and the skirt front right sides together, lining up the side seams. Match each seam intersection so the tiers flow from front to back, and sew along the two side seams. Finish the seam allowances together at ⅜ in (1 cm) and trim off the excess. Press the side seams flat.

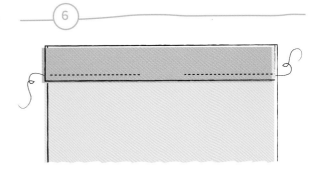

6 To form the waist, fold down ½ in (1.25 cm) around the top of the first tier and press. Fold another 1 in (2.5 cm) and press again. Stitch along the inside fold, leaving a 2-in (5-cm) opening.

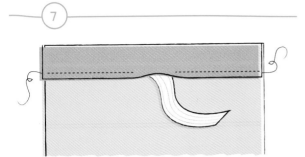

Cut the elastic to fit comfortably around your waist, plus an additional 1 in (2.5 cm) for overlapping in the next step. Attach a bodkin to one end and feed it through the opening left from Step 6.

Work the elastic around the waist and pull both ends out of the opening. Overlap 1 in (2.5 cm) and stitch with a zigzag stitch. Go back and forth a few times to secure the join, then feed the elastic back into the hole and stitch it closed.

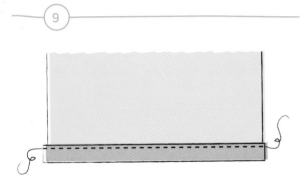

Press the hem of the skirt up by ½ in (1.25 cm), wrong sides together. Press up another ½ in (1.25 cm) and pin in place. Topstitch the hem as close to the inside fold as possible.

OTHER STYLES TO TRY

PRINT MIXING

Try your hand at combining three different fabrics by using one for each layer of the skirt. Sticking to a theme can be helpful—for example, by choosing three floral prints, three graphic prints, or the same print in three different colors.

OMBRE EFFECT

Got a favorite color? Make the skirt up in three shades of the same hue! Going from light to dark is a flattering choice, as the dark bottom will ground the skirt with a visual weight, drawing the eye down the body.

Like this style?
Check out the circle skirt on page 78.

THE TUNIC DRESS

The great thing about wearing a tunic dress is that it's as comfy and casual as your pajamas, but it's real-world accepted! This tunic is a chic take on what could be a frumpy dress, and looks great when paired with tights, leggings, or skinny jeans.

Sweeten it up with a feminine fabric choice, or make yours minimal and modern in solid black. However you decide to wear it, though, I guarantee you will be reaching for this tunic all the time.

Key characteristics
Typically, a tunic has a yoke in the front, and this version is no exception. Short raglan sleeves (which have slanted seams running from the underarm to the neckline) are attached to a full dress that is gathered into the yoke. As most tunics are not meant to be full-length dresses, this version is short and intended to be worn with something underneath it.

Who does it suit?
Pretty much all ages, tastes, and body sizes can wear this dress. Keep in mind that it hangs from the gathers below the yoke, so if you are full in the bust it will hang from that point of your body.

Suitable fabrics
Because of the drape of the dress, avoid stiff and heavy fabrics. Look for lightweight woven fabrics with good drape, like cotton voile, cotton lawn, double gauze, rayon, or silk. Just remember that slippery fabrics are harder to work with, so if you are a new sewer, try it with a cotton blend first.

Styling tips
If you're feeling sassy, wear your tunic over some opaque tights; otherwise try it over leggings or skinny jeans. Make it in a silk floral and play up its sweet side, or wear it with leggings and flats. It's not formal wear, so it's ideal for your day off, over your swimsuit, or for a casual day of shopping.

MAKING A TUNIC DRESS

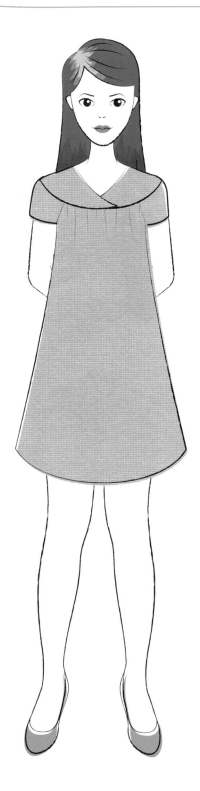

YOU WILL NEED
- 2¾ yds (2.5 m) lightweight woven fabric, 45 in (115 cm) wide
- Thread

GETTING STARTED
Refresh your gathering skills by reading up on it in Chapter 1 (see page 20). Practice on some scrap fabric first if it's your first time, and remember to keep your basting stitches on ⅜ in (1 cm) and ¾ in (2 cm) so that when you sew at the ⅝-in (1.5-cm) seam allowance, your stitches will go between the basting. And don't be skimpy on pins—it's a good idea to secure the layers when sewing.

PATTERN PIECES
301 = dress front (cut 1 on fold)
302 = dress back (cut 1 on fold)
303 = sleeve (cut 2)
304 = yoke back (cut 2 on fold)
305 = yoke front (cut 4)

TIP
When sewing your basting stitches, remember to keep the threads at the start and end of each stitch nice and long. This will make it easier to grab hold of them for the gathering!

Download your pattern here: http://bit.ly/U9iIX6

Place the dress front and the dress back pieces right sides together and line up the side seams. Sew along both sides, then finish the seams and press the seam allowances open.

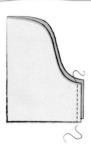

Fold the left sleeve right sides together and line up the short seam. Stitch, finish the seam, and press the seam allowance open. Repeat with the right sleeve.

Fold the hem of the sleeve up ½ in (1.25 cm), wrong sides together, and press. Repeat and topstitch close to the inside fold. Repeat with the other sleeve.

Finish the seam allowances together at ⅜ in (1 cm) with a zigzag stitch, and trim off the extra seam allowance. Press the seam allowance down.

Turn the sleeves right side out and the dress wrong side out. Insert the sleeves into the opening. Line up the side seams and stitch the U-shaped armhole openings. Make sure you sew the right sleeve to the right side and the left sleeve to the left side by matching notches.

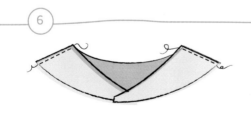

Place one set of the yoke front pieces on one of the yoke back pieces. Line up the shoulder seams and sew together. Press the seams open. Repeat with the other set of yoke front and back pieces so you have two identical sets.

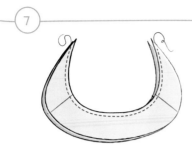

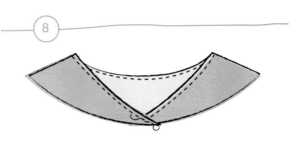

Place the yoke sets right sides together and line up the inside curve that is the neckline opening. Stitch together. Zigzag the seam allowances together at ⅜ in (1 cm) and trim off the extra.

Flip the yoke pieces right sides out with wrong sides together. Press the seam stitched in Step 7 so it is flat, and topstitch ¼ in (0.7 cm) from the seam edge. Fold the pieces so the fronts are in the front and baste them together where they meet.

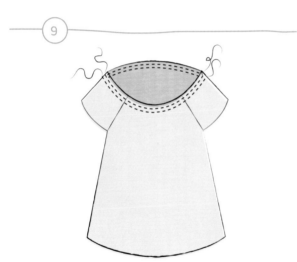

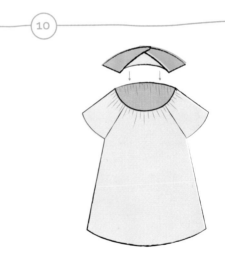

Sew two rows of basting stitches across the dress front at the ⅜-in (1-cm) and ¾-in (2-cm) seam allowances. Start and stop at the sides of the sleeves. Repeat on the dress back.

Turn the yoke right side out and the dress wrong side out. Insert the yoke into the opening. Line up the center of the dress front with the center front of the yoke, and the center back of the dress with the center back of the yoke. Gather the dress to fit the yoke. Stitch the yoke to the dress and remove the basting stitches.

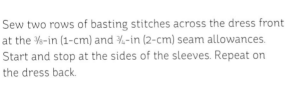

Finish the seam allowances together at ⅜ in (1 cm) with a zigzag stitch. Trim off the extra seam allowance and press down toward the dress. Fold the hem of the dress up ½ in (1.25 cm), wrong sides together, and press. Press another ½ in (1.25 cm), and stitch close to the inside fold.

OTHER STYLES TO TRY

YOKE EMBROIDERY

The yoke area around the neck can be a perfect spot to feature some embellishment, such as embroidery. Try some of the stitches in Chapter 3 to customize your tunic. If you need to draw the design on first, be sure to use a water-soluble marking tool that you've tested on a scrap first.

COLOR BLOCKING

Cut the yoke in a color or print that contrasts with the rest of the dress. Try two prints or two solids, or mix a solid and a print. When you sew your own clothes, you're in charge.

Like this style?
Check out the baby doll dress on page 60.

THE SMOCKED SUNDRESS

I love a good easy, breezy sundress, and there's a wonderful nostalgic feeling to a smocked sundress—it is weirdly timeless. You would think it would be too retro referential, but its appeal just keeps going. One of the great things about this dress is that anyone can wear it and instantly feel ready for a summer picnic.

Unlike some other classic shapes, this dress really is meant for leisure and is best in that type of setting. It is inherently flirty and girly, and if you pick a fun and retro fabric, you can take that theme a long way.

Key characteristics
The main element of this dress is the smocked shirring of the bodice. This effect is created with elastic thread and gives the bodice stretch, so it will fit a variety of shapes. After the elastic panel the dress flows down to just above the knee in a gathered rectangle.

Who does it suit?
This dress truly fits any shape and size, but you do need to be comfortable with an extremely fitted bodice. It is elastic, so it is forgiving and will move with you, but it will be fitted to your body at all times. Since there are no sleeves, you also need to be happy about exposing your arms.

Suitable fabrics
Because of the shirring, the fabric needs to be lightweight or else it will not gather up correctly. A cotton quilt weight on the heavy side of the spectrum, or a cotton voile on the lightweight side of things, is just about right.

Styling tips
You can really play up the retro vintage girly elements of this dress. Consider how adorable it would look made up in a red-and-white picnic gingham, or a 1950s-inspired floral. The shoulders have tied bows, so keep that in mind when choosing to layer over it with a cardigan, as there might be bulk to contend with.

Smocked polka dot dress by La Redoute.

MAKING A SMOCKED SUNDRESS

YOU WILL NEED
- 2⅛ yds (2 m) lightweight woven fabric, 45 in (115 cm) wide
- Thread
- Elastic thread

GETTING STARTED
Make sure you have all the proper tools for this project—especially water-soluble chalk pencils. All the shirring rows will be drawn on the right side of the fabric so that the bobbin's elastic thread is on the inside. But you will want these marks to go away, so do test the chalk on your fabric before starting!

PATTERN PIECES
401 = dress front and back (cut 2 on fold)
402 = shoulder ties (cut 4)

TIP
The key to using elastic thread in the machine is winding it onto the bobbin by hand. Do not stretch it while winding, but do not leave it loose either. Finding the perfect balance and winding it on nice and evenly is the key. You will likely run out during the shirring process, too. You don't want this to happen during a row, so keep your eye on the bobbin, and reload it between rows of sewing.

Download your pattern here:
http://bit.ly/1qznmly

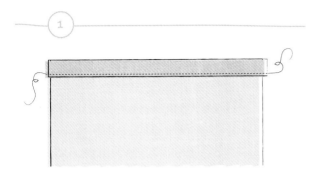

1

Fold the top of the dress front and back down ¼ in (0.7 cm), wrong sides together. Fold and press another ¼ in and pin in place. Topstitch as close to the inside fold as possible. Repeat on the bottom of the dress.

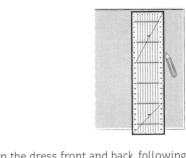

2

On the dress front and back, following the markings on the pattern, draw the lines for the elastic thread shirring on the dress front and back. Use a water-soluble marking tool and test it on a scrap first.

3

Wind elastic thread on your machine's bobbin by hand. Do not stretch while winding and try to be even and distribute the thread equally on the bobbin.

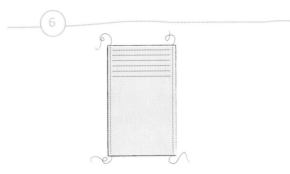

4

Using a regular straight stitch setting on your machine, sew along the lines you drew in Step 2 on both the front and back of the dress. Sew on the right side of the fabric so the elastic from the bobbin is on the inside of the dress. Do not backstitch, and leave long threads for both the main thread and the elastic thread so that when sewing the side seams, they will be locked in place.

5

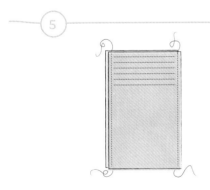

Place the dress front and back pieces wrong sides together and pin along the sides. Change the bobbin thread back to regular thread, then sew the side seams at the ⅜-in (1-cm) seam allowance, then trim the seams down to ⅛ in (0.3 cm).

6

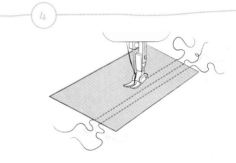

Turn the dress right sides together and sew along the side seams at ¼ in (0.7 cm) to form a French seam.

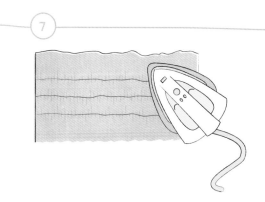

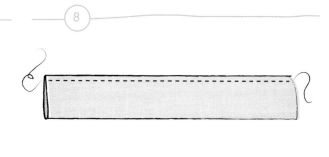

Set your iron to a high steam setting and hover it over the shirring. Press the steam button as you hover and the water and heat will shrink the elastic threads. Shrink as much or as little as you desire, but be sure to rotate the dress so you shrink it up equally.

Fold the four strap pieces in half, right sides together. Sew the long ends at the ⅜-in (1-cm) seam allowance. Trim the seam allowances down to ⅛ in (0.3 cm).

Attach a safety pin to one end of a strap piece and feed it into the tube to help you turn the tube right side out. This can be fussy so be patient! After you have turned it, remove the pin and press the strap flat, then fold under and press ¼ in (0.7 cm) at one end of the strap. Repeat for the other straps.

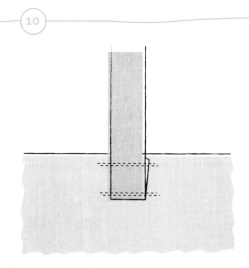

Try the dress on without the straps and mark where you would like them to be. Take it off and insert the straps into the dress by 1 in (2.5 cm), folded side down. Stitch them in place with a stitch at the fold and at the top of the intersection of the strap and the dress. Tie little knots on the ends of each strap, then tie the straps into bows at the shoulders to wear.

OTHER STYLES TO TRY

BOTTOM RUFFLE

Adding a ruffle to the hem of the dress is easy and the effect is adorable. Simply measure the width of the front panel, then add on half that number. So if the panel width is 20 in (50 cm), the total width of your ruffle will be 30 in (75 cm). The height can be anything you like, but add a ⅝-in (1.5-cm) seam allowance for sewing it to the dress, and 1 in (2.5 cm) for a double-fold hem at the bottom.

Simply cut two of these panels, sew them right sides together along the sides, then gather the top and sew it to the bottom of the dress. Easy!

MAKE IT BLOUSY

If you'd prefer the bodice more blousy, you can simply skip a bunch of the shirring lines in the middle of the bodice. Draw the top few and the bottom few shirring lines, and only sew the elastic thread along those marks. The dress will then be fitted at the top and at the waist, but the fabric in between will be open.

Like this style?
Check out the tunic dress on page 48.

Opposite: Jersey knit dress by
Chie Duncan (tl); Floral dress by
Christine Battaglia (bl); Floral
dress by Free People, styled by
Kayley Anne (r). **Above:** Floral
dress by Free People styled by
Kayley Anne (t); Blue beaded
vintage fabric and wool dress,
by Karine Bono (b).

THE BABY DOLL DRESS

A baby doll dress can conjure up memories of certain style icons from the past—Courtney Love, Twiggy, and Mia Farrow, to name a few. But this silhouette can be fun and modern as well. I love the wearability of something completely loose through the body, but the beauty of this garment is that it still retains elements of tailoring, creating the ultimate yin and yang.

You can play with accessories to change the look of this garment. Tights will cover your legs and keep things lean and long, while knee-high socks will give it a preppy look. So be mindful of your style intentions and fabric choices, depending on where you want to take your new dress!

Key characteristics
One of the key elements of a good baby doll dress is that while the lower half of the body is completely bare, the upper half is demure and covered. This version is designed with a simple neckline, full-length gathered sleeves, and a gathered yoke at the bust—all standard elements for this style of dress.

Who does it suit?
This is best worn by those who feel really comfortable baring a lot of leg! You can wear tights to keep things opaque, but your legs will still be out there for all the world to see, so keep that in mind.

Suitable fabrics
To keep the shape of the dress soft and flowing, stick to fabrics that are quilt-weight woven cotton and lighter. This can be made up in silk, rayon, or lightweight cottons, but it's not advisable to make it from something stiff or crisp.

Styling tips
Decide how little girly you want to go and run with it! Playing it up? Pair the dress with knee-high socks, Mary Jane flats, and a handbag. Playing it down? Wear it with tights, boots, and a cardigan over the top.

MAKING A BABY DOLL DRESS

YOU WILL NEED

- 3⅓ yds (3 m) lightweight woven fabric, 45 in (115 cm) wide
- 1 yd (90 cm) double-fold bias tape
- Thread

GETTING STARTED

When choosing a size, keep the upper portion of your body in mind, as the rest of this garment is meant to be big and flowing. Focus on fitting the shoulders and upper chest, and let the rest of it hang loose and free.

PATTERN PIECES

501 = bodice front (cut 1 on fold)
502 = bodice back (cut 1 on fold)
503 = skirt front (cut 1 on fold)
504 = skirt back (cut 1 on fold)
505 = sleeve (cut 2)
506 = sleeve cuff (cut 2 on fold)

TIP

This dress uses bias tape and gathering, both of which are covered in Chapter 1. If you're unsure about either of these skills, read up on them, and practice on a piece of scrap fabric before cutting the material for your finished dress.

Download your pattern here:
http://bit.ly/1m9T6Qr

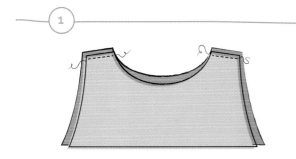

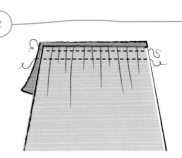

Place the yoke front and yoke back together, right sides facing. Pin along the shoulder seams and stitch. Finish the seam allowance as you like, and then press the seams open.

Sew basting stitches along the top of the skirt front at ⅜ in (1 cm) and ¾ in (2 cm) and gather to match the front yoke hem. Stitch right sides together, remove the basting, then zigzag the seams together at ⅜ in (1 cm). Trim, then press the seam allowance toward the bodice. Repeat with the back yoke and back skirt piece.

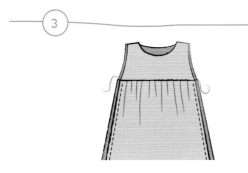

Place the dress front and the dress back right sides together. Pin the side seams and stitch. Finish the seam allowances as you like and press the seams open.

Sew basting stitches along both the right and left sleeve caps at ⅜ in (1 cm) and ¾ in (2 cm). Fold each sleeve in half, right sides together, and sew along the side seam. Finish the seam allowances and press the seams open.

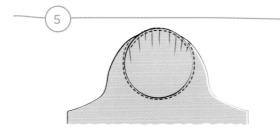

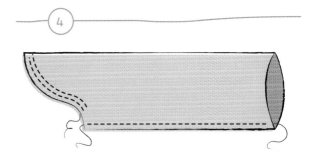

Turn the sleeves right side out and the dress wrong side out. Fit the sleeves into the armhole openings, lining up raw edges and notches, and matching side seams. Gather the sleeves to fit, pin in place, and sew. Zigzag the seam allowances together at ⅜ in (1 cm), trim, and press the seam allowance toward the sleeves.

Fold one cuff piece in half and stitch the short ends together. Repeat on the other cuff piece. Press the seam allowance open.

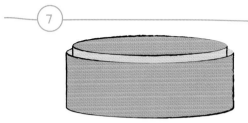

Fold the cuff pieces in half, wrong sides together, matching the raw edges at the end opposite the fold. Press the fold flat.

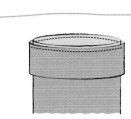

Baste each sleeve hem at ⅜ in (1 cm) and ¾ in (2 cm), then gather to the cuff diameter. With the sleeves right side out, slip the cuff over the sleeve hem. Line up the raw edges, adjust the gathers, then pin and stitch. Remove the basting stitches, finish with a zigzag stitch through both layers at ⅜ in (1 cm), and trim.

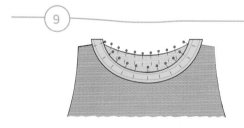

Open one fold of the bias tape and pin it to the neckline, right sides together. Start at the center back and work your way right around. Pin the two ends together where they meet, right sides together, and sew with a straight stitch. Trim off the excess tape, press the seam flat, and re-pin to the neckline of the dress.

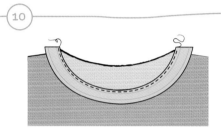

Sew the tape to the neckline in the valley of the fold closest to the neck opening. Trim the seam allowance in half.

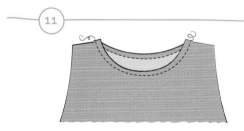

Fold the bias tape to the inside of the neck opening, tucking the seam allowance into the center of the tape. Fold again until all the tape is on the inside and only the dress fabric is showing around the neck. Stitch the tape to the neckline on the inside of the dress, as close to the outer fold as possible. This will also show as topstitching on the right side of the neckline.

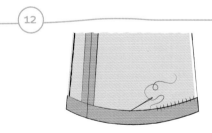

Press the hem of the dress up by ½ in (1.25 cm), wrong sides together, then press another ½ in (1.25 cm). Pin in place, then topstitch the hem as close to the inside fold as possible, or sew in place with a hand stitch.

OTHER STYLES TO TRY

PATCH POCKETS

Is there anything more appealing than a patch pocket? Well, maybe, but I think we can all agree that patch pockets are really darn cute. Try making one in a fun shape, like a circle or a heart, and attaching it to the side of the front of the dress. Make a pair or just one—it's your dress, so customize it how you want!

TRIM DETAILS

Adding fun trim like rickrack or lace is a lovely way to add some detail to an otherwise basic fabric selection. Sew some trim in a few rows at the hem of the skirt, at the hem of the sleeves, or around the neckline.

Like this style?
Check out the shift dress on page 96.

THE UPCYCLED T-SHIRT DRESS

When you begin to sew your own clothing, the nature of ethics comes up naturally, since sewing itself raises questions of handmade versus store-bought—which leads to thinking about who made that store-bought item, and on and on. Learning to take some goodies from a thrift store, or from the depths of your own closet, is a fun and rewarding way to recycle.

If you like the coziness of wearing a T-shirt, then you're going to love making that T-shirt into a dress. It feels like cheating, because it is like wearing your pajamas out in public and getting away with it. You'll never look at used items the same way again!

Key characteristics
The main elements here are two T-shirts; one that fits you, and one that is far too big for you. The top half is fitted, and the lower half is a gathered skirt, but you are in control of where the two meet, so you can place this junction at the most flattering part of your upper body.

Who does it suit?
This is the kind of dress that pretty much suits everyone. The only thing to consider, if you are slightly larger than average, is that you will need to find a T-shirt that is larger than your widest measurement below the bust.

Suitable fabrics
Restricting your search to either stable 100 percent cotton knits, or a cotton and lycra blend, is best. Really drapey rayon knits and silk knits are lovely, but much fussier to work with. Also avoid choosing something heavy, like a sweatshirt knit, which will be extremely bulky at the waist.

Styling tips
Depending on the T-shirt you choose, this dress can go in a number of ways. Choose an old favorite concert T-shirt for the top and the whole thing gets instantly casual. But pick a classic black knit and it will be much more classic.

Opposite: Black T-shirt dress by Keren Zarka. **Above:** T-shirt dress by Esther Richardson, styled by Jenna Richardson (t); Blue short-sleeved T-shirt dress by Keren Zarka (b).

MAKING AN UPCYCLED T-SHIRT DRESS

YOU WILL NEED

- A T-shirt that fits your upper body and is at least as long as your natural waist
- A T-shirt that is at least a few inches wider than your hip
- 1½ yds (1.4 m) elastic, ½ in (1.25 cm) wide
- Thread
- 80/12 or 70/11 ball-point needles for sewing knit fabrics

GETTING STARTED

The key to this dress is finding the right T-shirts for the two halves of the dress. Try to find fabrics of similar content and weight so that the fabric is consistent where they meet at the waist.

TIP
When searching for the lower, wider portion of the dress, check out the men's section at your local thrift shore!

1

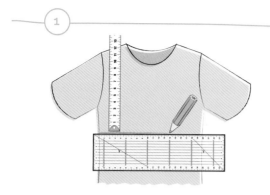

Measure down from the shoulder to where you want the skirt to be attached. Add ½ in (1.25 cm) to the measurement for the seam allowance for sewing on the skirt, then draw a line across the T-shirt at this point.

2

Cut along the line drawn in Step 1 to create the top half of the T-shirt dress. Discard the lower half of the T-shirt.

3

On the T-shirt to be used for the skirt portion, draw a line across the shirt just under the sleeve. Cut along that line to create the bottom half of the dress.

4

Measure the opening at the bottom of the top and add 1 in (2.5 cm) to this measurement. Cut a piece of elastic to this length. Overlap the ends of the elastic by ½ in (1.25 cm) and sew them together with a zigzag stitch. Go back and forth a few times to secure the join.

5

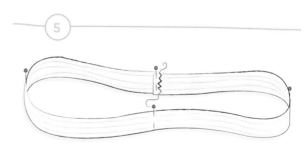

Divide the circle of elastic into four equal parts and mark each spot with a pin.

6

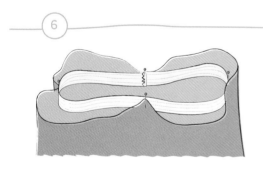

Insert the circle of elastic into the top of the skirt. Divide the top of the skirt portion into four equal parts and pin the elastic in place at each spot.

Select a zigzag stitch and insert the elastic and skirt into your machine at one of the pinned spots. Lower the presser foot and sink the needle into the elastic. Stretch the elastic from the needle to the first pin, matching the length of the skirt. Sew your way around the whole skirt, keeping the zigzag stitches near the top of the elastic so that there is a little room to the left of the stitches on the elastic.

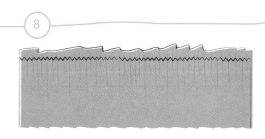

After you've gone all the way around, the skirt will be gathered up into the elastic and ready to be attached to the top half of the dress.

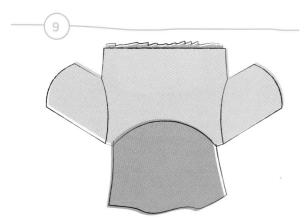

Turn the skirt right side out and the top half wrong side out. Slip the skirt portion through the neck opening and line up the raw edges around the top of the skirt and the bottom of the top. Because the elastic was cut to fit the top, the skirt should now be the same size as the top. Pin in place.

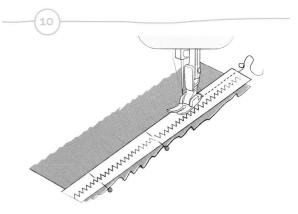

Just underneath the zigzag stitching, but remaining on the elastic, stitch the skirt to the top with a straight stitch. Because the elastic has been gathered with the zigzag, the straight stitches will not snap when the dress is put on or taken off.

OTHER STYLES TO TRY

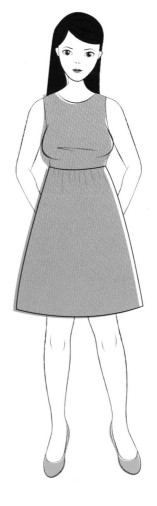

SKIRT POCKETS

You could use scraps from the sleeves of the T-shirt chosen for the bottom to make some patch pockets for the skirt. Or, if you want a third fabric, find a T-shirt with pockets on it. Remove the pockets and sew them onto your skirt. Why not? They're already made!

TANK DRESS

There is no need to limit yourself to just T-shirts for the top half of the dress. Mix it up and choose an upcycled tank top. Both tight and loose versions would work just fine, depending on how fitted or breezy you'd like your dress to be.

Like this style?
Check out the upcycled men's shirt skirt on page 114.

THE SLEEVELESS SHEATH DRESS

The sheath dress is such a timeless garment. It spans ages and tastes, and shows up in every circle. This is because it looks good on everyone, and is a blank canvas just waiting to be directed by the wearer. Pretty much everyone can wear this dress, and it is appropriate in almost every situation.

Typically, the sheath is fitted at the waist, but for that to be perfect, there is quite a lot of pattern fitting to be done. Since this book is for the first-time sewer, the dress I have designed here is a little looser, ensuring a wearable success as you hone your sewing skills.

Key characteristics
The classic shape of the sheath is an hourglass—a fuller bust, smaller waist, and fuller hip. The shaping of the waist is thanks to a pair of contour darts, which nip in the fabric at the most flattering place. Fitted versions often have a zipper up the back. Looser styles, as here, pull on over the head.

Who does it suit?
Just about anyone. The outlines of the shape move around those with curves, and it can create curves for bodies that don't have any. Sheath dresses can be sleeveless, or can have sleeves anywhere from very short to wrist length.

Suitable fabrics
Since this dress has no gathers or spots of fullness, fabrics can go from very lightweight, like silk or cotton voile, to slightly heavy, like a cotton or linen canvas. However, a thicker fabric will result in a stiffer dress, which will be slightly more difficult to get on and off over your head.

Styling tips
In an understated fabric, the sheath can be dressed up retro Jackie O style, with a cardigan, flats, and a pillbox hat. Or, if you've picked a classic gingham, it will be perfect for a walk in the park with sandals and a picnic basket.

Opposite: Colorblock sheath dress by Miss Selfridge (tl); Daisy jacquard dress by Dunnes Stores (bl); French terry jersey dress by Nancy Dee Brooke (r). **Above:** Blue crochet dress by Dunnes Stores (t); African print cotton dress by Solome Katongole (b).

MAKING A SLEEVELESS SHEATH DRESS

YOU WILL NEED
- 2⅓ yds (2.2 m) lightweight to medium-weight woven fabric, 45 in (115 cm) wide
- 3 yds (2.75 m) double-fold bias tape
- Thread

GETTING STARTED
If you've selected a heavier fabric for the dress, I would suggest picking a lighter fabric for the bias tape at the neck and armholes, as folding a heavier fabric will prove to be difficult and bulky.

PATTERN PIECES
601 = dress front (cut 1 on fold)
602 = dress back (cut 1 on fold)

TIP
Because this dress is designed to pull on over the head, don't get set on making it in a smaller size to create a more fitted version, or you will have great difficulty getting it on and off! This dress is designed to be a less-fitted version of the sheath, so choose your size accordingly.

Download your pattern here:
http://bit.ly/1jHwAE1

1

Sew the bust darts and press them down toward the hem of the dress.

2

Sew the contour darts on the back of the dress. Snip the center of the darts and press them toward the side seams.

3

Place the dress front and dress back together, right sides facing. Pin the shoulder seams together and stitch. Finish the seam allowances as you prefer, and press the seams open.

4

With the dress front and dress back still right sides together, stitch along the side seams. Finish the seam allowances as you prefer, and press the seams open.

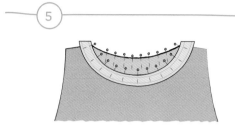

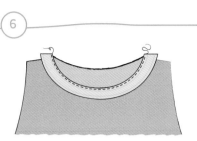

Open one fold of the bias tape and pin it to the neckline, right sides together. Start at the center back and work your way around. Pin the two ends together where they meet, right sides together, and sew with a straight stitch. Trim off the excess tape, press the seam flat, then re-pin the center back tape to the dress's neckline.

Sew the tape to the neckline in the valley of the fold closest to the neck opening. Trim the seam allowance in half.

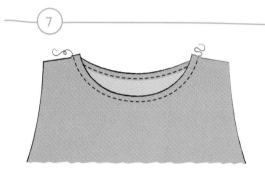

Fold the bias tape to the inside of the neck opening, tucking the seam allowance into the center of the tape. Fold again until all the tape is on the inside and only the dress fabric is showing around the neck. Stitch the tape to the neckline on the inside of the dress, as close to the outer fold as possible. This will also show as topstitching on the right side of the neckline.

Repeat this process for each of the armhole openings.

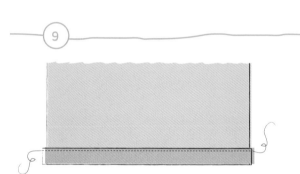

Press the hem of the dress up by ½ in (1.25 cm), wrong sides together, then press another ½ in (1.25 cm). Pin in place, then topstitch the hem as close to the inside fold as possible.

OTHER STYLES TO TRY

LILLY IT

Take after the master, Lilly Pulitzer, and add some vintage trim down the center front and along the hem. This kind of wide trim is best applied by hand, so after completing the dress, take your time hand-sewing it for some major vintage flair.

EYELET OR LACE

Make up the dress using eyelet or lace and pair with a pretty vintage slip underneath. Use the border of the lace or eyelet at the hem for a fancy touch and a hem that doesn't need to be sewn!

Like this style?
Check out the shift dress on page 96.

THE CIRCLE SKIRT

A true circle skirt has an outer circle, which becomes the hem, and an inner circle, which becomes the waist. Many so-called circle skirts out there are, in fact, half-circles, three-quarter circles, or any other percentage of a real circle. These look similar to a true circle skirt, but are simply less full.

The version I've designed here is short and sweet, reminiscent of a skater skirt. The flounce is undeniably flirty and youthful, making any outfit sweeter. The real challenge with this skirt is working with all the curves, but take your time and remember you can always practice before you cut and sew the real version.

Key characteristics
The main element of this skirt is the circle itself. This kind of cut will create fullness and folds in the fabric, all the while keeping a smooth line from the waist to the hem. A circle skirt achieves this fullness because of the circle, rather than any gathering or pleating.

Who does it suit?
Circle skirts can come in any length, but this version is quite short, so it is best for someone comfortable showing a lot of leg. Since the skirt nips in at the waist and flows to the hem, it is also best suited to those whose waist measurement is smaller than their hip measurement.

Suitable fabrics
This version of the circle skirt has an elastic waist, creating a few gathers at the top. That, in addition to the flounce of the skirt, means that it is best sewn in a lightweight woven fabric, such as quilting-weight cotton, cotton voile, or lightweight linen.

Styling tips
This skirt is rather youthful so it's best to balance that with something classic and demure. Consider a fitted top and cardigan to top off the flounce of the skirt. And since it's rather short, pairing it with tights and flats keeps the whole look elegant.

MAKING A CIRCLE SKIRT

YOU WILL NEED

- 2 yds (1.9 m) lightweight woven fabric, 60 in (150 cm) wide
- 6 yds (5.5 m) double-fold bias tape
- 1½ yds (1.4 m) elastic, ¾ in (2 cm) wide
- Thread

GETTING STARTED

It will take a good deal of room to spread out the fabric and the pattern, since you need to accommodate the full circle of the skirt's shape. If your cutting table is too small, try clearing a spot on the floor. Note that non-carpeted floors will be much easier to cut on, so find a carpet-free spot if you can!

PATTERN PIECES

701 = skirt front and back (cut 2 on fold)

TIP

Take your time when you are working the bias tape around the waist and hem. Since the skirt has such a curve, the hem cannot simply be folded in and stitched because the outer circle going up will be larger than the inner circle it's being folded into. That is why we sew bias tape to the hem—it will curve with the shape of the skirt.

Download your pattern here:
http://bit.ly/1qXHshv

1

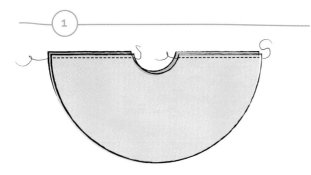

Lay the front and back skirt pieces right sides together. Pin the side seams and sew them with a straight stitch. Finish the seams by sewing the seam allowances together with a zigzag stitch at ⅜ in (1 cm). Trim off the excess fabric and press the seams flat.

4

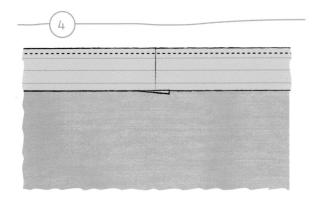

Pin the raw end on top of the folded end, which will hide it in the next step, then stitch the bias tape to the waist with a ⅜-in (1-cm) seam allowance.

2

Open the bias tape and press the center fold and one outer fold flat. Fold one short end of the bias tape over by ¼ in (0.7 cm), wrong sides together, and press. Stitch in place close to the raw end of the fold.

3

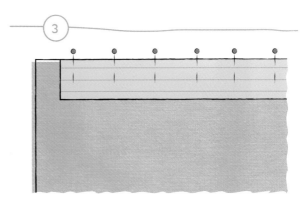

Pin the bias tape to the waist, right sides together, matching the raw edge of the bias tape to the top of the skirt. Start with the end that you stitched in Step 2, then work around the skirt waist until the bias meets up with the start.

5

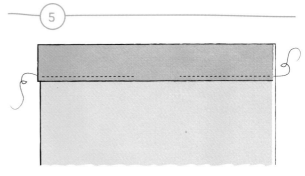

Trim the seam allowance down to ⅛ in (0.3 cm), then fold the bias tape to the inside of the skirt, wrong sides together. Press, pin, then stitch along the inside fold, stopping 2 in (5 cm) before the start of the stitch to leave a 2-in (5-cm) opening.

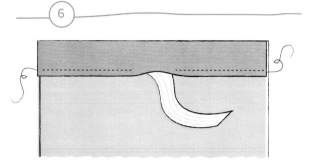

Cut a length of elastic to fit comfortably around your waist, plus an additional 1 in (2.5 cm) for overlapping in the next step. Attach a bodkin to the end, then feed it into the hole left in the fold in Step 5.

Work the elastic around the waist and pull both ends out of the opening. Overlap these by 1 in (2.5 cm) and stitch with a zigzag stitch. Go back and forth a few times to secure the join. Feed the elastic back into the hole and stitch closed.

8

Repeat Steps 2 to 5 on the hem of the skirt, but without leaving an opening for elastic. Stitch along the inside fold all around the hem and press again.

OTHER STYLES TO TRY

CONTRAST BIAS TAPE

Even though it's on the inside of the skirt, try using a contrasting fabric for the bias tape on the hem, so when people catch a glimpse of the inside at one of the flounces, they'll get a happy surprise!

CREATE A BORDER PRINT

This skirt is a blank canvas, just waiting to be customized. Try drawing a design—or iron one on—to follow with embroidery floss to create a custom print along the hem of the skirt.

Like this style?
Check out the wrap skirt on page 120.

Opposite: Embellished floral slip dress by Miss Selfridge. **Above:** V-neck slip dress by Wallis (t); Slip dress by Pachamama Bali, styled by Jenna Richardson (b).

THE SLIP DRESS

There's no way around it—the slip dress is sexy. It walks a fine line and begs a lot of questions: Is it a dress? Is it a slip? Is it meant to be worn out? Is it meant to be worn only at home? However you choose to wear it, be ready for these kinds of looks because it is one sexy number.

There are ways to make it less so, though. For example, tame its otherwise sexy silhouette by pairing it with flat sandals and a cardigan, and it's ready for a casual date. Or, you can reserve it for wearing in the privacy of your own home, saving it as a fancy pajama.

Key characteristics
A slip dress is modeled after a full slip—traditionally a slim-fitting garment with thin straps, typically worn under a dress to keep it from being too sheer, or from clinging to undergarments. A slip dress is usually floor length, but as slips themselves come in various lengths, so can the slip dress. And much like slips, the dress version comes in both straight-grain and bias-cut versions.

Who does it suit?
As this is a straight-grain version and not cut on the bias (which is much harder for a beginner to sew), the drape of the dress falls from the bust to the floor. If you are busty, it will hang from the widest point and will be very full. From the bust point to the hem, it is cut like an A-line, allowing for a fuller hip.

Suitable fabrics
This is best made in lightweight and flowy fabrics, with little to no stiffness. Silk, cotton voile, cotton lawn, Swiss dot, and rayon are the best choices to keep it full and flowing.

Styling tips
Like the maxi skirt (page 42), there is built-in drama, thanks to the length of the dress. It is easy to wear to the beach over a bathing suit and tank top, or you can pair it with a belt and heels and hit the town. It's very open at the top, so a cardigan or another layer can help if covering up is a concern.

MAKING A SLIP DRESS

YOU WILL NEED
- 3 yds (2.75 m) lightweight woven fabric, 45 in (115 cm) wide
- 3 yds (2.75 m) double-fold bias tape
- Thread

GETTING STARTED
If you choose to make up this dress in silk or rayon, consider using a slightly more stable fabric, like cotton, for the bias tape. Or purchase bias tape made from a silky fabric so the work is done for you!

PATTERN PIECES
801 = dress front (cut 1 on fold)
802 = dress back (cut 1 on fold)

TIP
The bias tape will act as the straps and the edging at the top of the dress on the front and the back, so consider that when choosing fabrics. The tape can be made of a different color, print, or fabric for a lovely accent.

Download your pattern here:
http://bit.ly/1m9QIJn

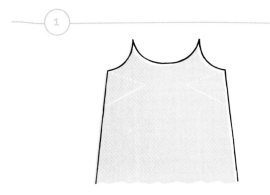

1

Sew the bust darts and press them down toward the hem of the dress.

2

Open up one fold on the bias tape and pin the raw edge to the top of the front dress, right sides together. Stitch in place by sewing in the fold closest to the raw edge. Repeat on the back of the dress.

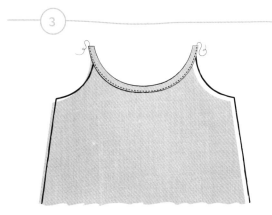

3

Fit the seam allowance into the center fold of the bias tape and fold half of the tape to the inside, so half is on the inside and half is on the outside. Stitch along the edge farthest from the neckline. Stitch on the right side of the dress so you can see your topstitching, but be sure to catch the back side of the bias tape at the same time. Repeat on the dress back.

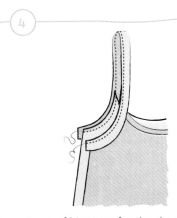

4

Cut two pieces of bias tape for the shoulder straps that fit your shoulders comfortably. Open one and pin it in place on one side of the dress as you did in Step 2. Stitch in place, fold, and stitch again as you did in Step 3, stitching around the shoulder strap and closing up the tape. Repeat on the other side of the dress.

Place the dress front and dress back wrong sides together. Check to make sure the straps are not twisted. Stitch the front and back pieces together along the side seams with a ⅜-in (1-cm) seam allowance.

Trim the seam allowance down to ⅛ in (0.3 cm). Turn the dress right sides together and press the side seams flat. Pin the seams in place and stitch the side seams at ¼ in (0.7 cm) to form a French seam (see also page 57).

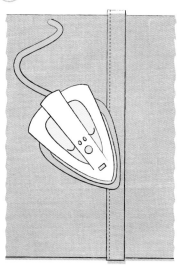

Press the seam allowances toward the back.

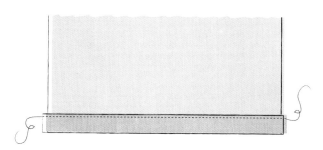

Press the hem of the dress up by ½ in (1.25 cm), wrong sides together, then press another ½ in (1.25 cm). Pin in place, then topstitch the hem as close to the inside fold as possible.

OTHER STYLES TO TRY

LACE TRIM

Play up the slip aspect of the dress by adding lace trim at the neckline and the hem. Look at some fancy slips and lingerie to get inspiration on placement. Take it one step further and tie ribbons into little bows and sew them on at the base of each strap.

CUT IT SHORT

Love the look but not into maxi-length dresses? No problem! Simply mark a new hem with chalk pencil, follow the original hemline to keep the shape right, and cut to your desired length to transform the slip into an easy summer sundress.

Like this style?
Check out the sleeveless sheath on page 72.

THE WRAP DRESS

Unlike some of the other classic shapes featured in this book, the wrap dress is somewhat open to interpretation, depending on the era and feel you are after. There is the polyester, Studio 54 version of the 1970s, there are the vintage and modern Diane von Furstenberg versions, and dozens more. When I think of the wrap dress, I focus on the ease of the garment, as well as the effortless wrap-and-go feel of the shape.

The style I have designed here is easy to make and wear, and is ideal for layering in the winter and wearing alone in the heat of the summer. I picture this worn with wedge espadrilles and large sunglasses like a 1970s girl around town, but it could also be modernized in no time with fun fabrics and chic accessories.

Key characteristics
This dress has a deep V-neck wrap in front, an A-line skirt, and ties that pass around the body at the natural waist. The front opening is finished with bias tape, running up from the hem, around the neck, and back down the other side.

Who does it suit?
This style is best on someone whose waist is smaller than their hip, as the cinching takes place at that point. Since the dress pieces must overlap, be sure you make a size large enough to wrap around your body.

Suitable fabrics
Stick to lightweight to medium-weight woven fabrics, as the A-line skirt and kimono sleeve will not take well to stiff fabrics. Quilt-weight cotton, lightweight linen, chambray cotton, and similar weight fabrics are perfect.

Styling tips
Because of the rather deep V-neck, not everyone will feel comfortable wearing this dress on its own, but that is exactly why I designed a short kimono-style sleeve—it will hang over a tight T-shirt or camisole perfectly! Team it with a long-sleeved top, tights, and boots in the cooler months, or try a pretty full slip when it's warmer.

Opposite: Pink wrap dress by F&F, styled by Jenna Richardson.
Above: Scallop-edged wrap dress by Anami and Janine (t); Patterned wrap dress by Warehouse, styled by Bex Hawkins (b).

MAKING A WRAP DRESS

YOU WILL NEED
- 3⅓ yds (3 m) lightweight to medium-weight woven fabric, 45 in (115 cm) wide
- 3 yds (2.75 m) double-fold bias tape
- Thread

GETTING STARTED
This dress has bound bias-tape edges around the front, so take some time making that element of the dress. Following the bias tape tutorial in Chapter 1 (see page 26), you can make your own custom trim in any fabric you like. Or, if you prefer, you can buy pre-made tape. Your choice!

PATTERN PIECES
901 = dress right front (cut 1)
902 = dress left front (cut 1)
903 = dress back (cut 1 on fold)
904 = waist tie (cut 2)

TIP
Since bias tape is cut on the bias, consider the print when choosing the fabric for your trim. Stripes and other linear prints look dynamic when cut on the bias, as the stripes will be on the diagonal of the bias tape, creating a wonderful graphic element around the dress opening.

Download your pattern here:
http://bit.ly/1mAlq1Y

1

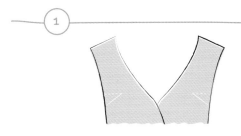

Sew the bust darts on the two dress front pieces and press the darts down toward the waist.

2

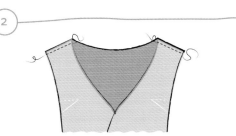

Place the dress back right side up. Place the two dress front pieces on top, right sides down, lining up the shoulders. Sew the dress fronts to the dress back along the shoulder seams. Finish the seam allowances as you prefer, and press the seams open.

3

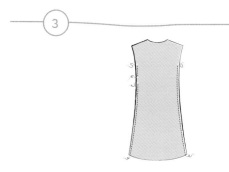

With the dress pieces right sides together, stitch the side seams from the hem to the dot under the arm. On the side with three dots, stitch from the hem to the first dot and secure with a backstitch. Leave the small distance between the two dots for the sash opening. Sew a backstitch at the top of the sash opening and continue sewing to the top dot under the arm.

4

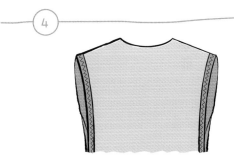

Press the side seams open from the hem to under the armhole. When you reach the armhole, continue pressing a ⅝-in (1.5-cm) seam allowance, folding the sleeve to the inside. Now finish the edges of the seam allowance with a zigzag stitch, but leave them untrimmed.

5

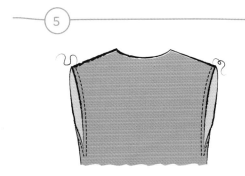

Stitch around the armhole openings, sewing close to the raw edge and pivoting under the armhole.

6

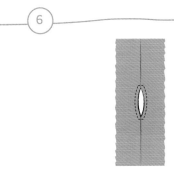

Sew around the small hole (sash opening) left in the side seam to keep the seam allowance in place.

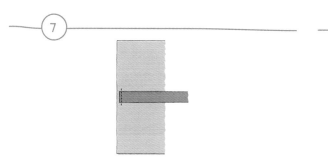

Fold the two waist ties, right sides together. Stitch the long side and one short end at the ⅜-in (1-cm) seam allowance. Turn the ties right side out, using a point turner or knitting needle to poke out the corners on the sewn end, and press flat. Pin the waist ties to the wrong side of the dress fronts, following the markings on the pattern. Baste in place at ⅜ in (1 cm).

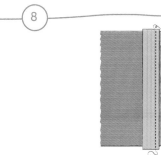

Open up one fold on the bias tape and pin the raw edge to the front of the dress, right sides together. Start at the hem, go up one side front, over the neck, and down the other side front to the hem. Stitch in place by sewing in the fold closest to the raw edge.

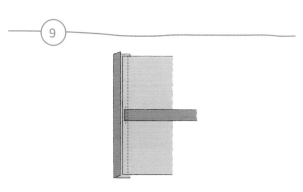

Fit the seam allowance into the center fold of the bias tape and fold half of the tape to the inside so that half is on the inside and half is on the outside.

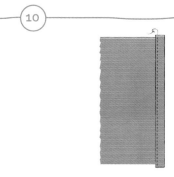

Stitch along the inside edge of the tape. Sew on the front side of the dress so you can see your topstitching, but be sure to catch the back side of the tape at the same time.

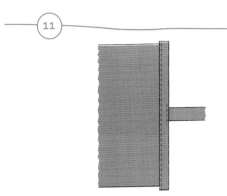

Fold the waist ties forward and secure them in place with a small stitch.

Press the hem of the skirt up by ½ in (1.25 cm), wrong sides together. Press another ½ in (1.25 cm) and pin in place. Fold the bias tape along with the hem and press well. Topstitch the hem as close to the inside fold as possible.

OTHER STYLES TO TRY

RETRO EMBROIDERY

If you are looking to play up the 1970s vibe of this dress, why not go all the way and embellish it with embroidery! Think of all those really great floral and bohemian designs that you could use around the hem, dress opening, and sleeve hem. Check out the tutorial on basic embroidery stitches in Chapter 3 (page 132).

CONTRASTING TRIM

As all the binding around the front of the dress is visible on the right side of the garment, try making the bias tape in a contrasting fabric for a gorgeous outline around the dress front. Finish the trim accent by using matching contrasting fabric for the waist ties.

Like this style?
Check out the wrap skirt on page 120.

THE SHIFT DRESS

When you are searching your closet for a comfortable yet stylish outfit, the shift dress is always a fantastic choice. Unlike the sheath dress, this dress is ever so slightly less tailored, as there are no contour darts in the middle to cinch it into your waist. This dress has more of an A-line shape, pitching away from your body as it spans to the hem.

Creating proper set-in sleeves can be challenging for beginner sewers, so I designed this version with a dress and sleeve all in one to give you sleeves without the headache of tailoring. But no one will be the wiser, and you will definitely impress in your new shift dress.

Key characteristics
The key to a shift dress is its easy, slightly A-line shape, falling from shoulder to hem. Usually a shift is cut above the knee—sometimes quite far above! This version has a full three-quarter-length sleeve that is gathered and cuffed.

Who does it suit?
Because of its full and untailored shape, this is suitable for a variety of body types. If you are fuller in the bust, consider how the fabric will hang from there, since this will create a tentlike effect. It is not easy to belt because of its fullness, so if you are unsure, drape your fabric choice from your bust and see how it hangs.

Suitable fabrics
This dress can handle a range of fabric weights, from a lightweight cotton voile to a medium quilt-weight cotton or linen. The thicker the fabric, though, the bulkier it will be around the gathers at the sleeve cuff. The dress has very few seams so it's a perfect for featuring a large print too—you won't have to cut it up into lots of small pieces.

Styling tips
You can make this dress playful or serious. Pair a black silk fabric and with black hosiery, heels, and a statement necklace for a more fancy affair, or try out a retro floral print to play up the mod aspect of this retro shape for a casual day out.

Opposite: Pink shift dress by Miss Selfridge (tl); Cotton knit mod print dress by Merrick White (bl); Print dress by Dressabelle, styled by Uli Chan (r). **Above:** Black pleated shift by La Redoute (t); Embroidered shift dress by La Redoute (b).

MAKING A SHIFT DRESS

YOU WILL NEED
- 2½ yds (2.3 m) lightweight to medium-weight woven fabric, 45 in (115 cm) wide
- 1 yd (1 m) double-fold bias tape
- Thread

GETTING STARTED
It is always good practice to wash your fabric prior to cutting and sewing it up, so if this is not part of your sewing routine, it's a good habit to get into. All fabric is produced with a starch on the outside, making it stiffer than it really is, and it can be challenging to see the real drape of the fabric in this state. Plus the fabric will likely shrink a little, so the finished garment may no longer fit!

PATTERN PIECES
1001 = dress front (cut 1 on fold)
1002 = dress back (cut 1 on fold)
1003 = sleeve cuff (cut 2 on fold)

 TIP
The cuff can be made in a larger size than the rest of the dress if you find that you need more room in the band around your arm. Simply cut the larger size of band and gather the sleeve to fit. It will result in a slightly less full gather at the cuff, but it is better that it fits your arm than not!

Download your pattern here:
http://bit.ly/1mNSR1J

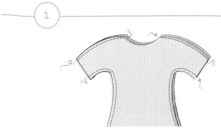

1

Place the dress front on the dress back, right sides together. Sew the shoulder seams with a straight stitch, then sew from the sleeve hem down to the dress hem along the side seams on both the right and left sides of the dress.

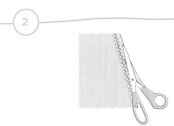

2

Finish the seams by sewing the seam allowances together with a zigzag stitch at ⅜ in (1 cm). Trim off the excess fabric and press the seams flat.

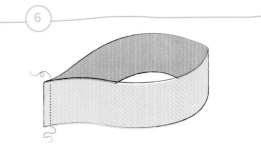

3

Open one fold of the bias tape and pin it to the neckline, right sides together. Start at the center back and work your way right around. Pin the two ends together where they meet, right sides together, and sew with a straight stitch. Trim off the excess tape, press the seam flat, and re-pin the center back tape to the dress's neckline.

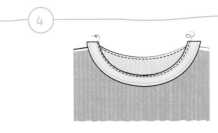

4

Sew the tape to the neckline in the valley of the fold closest to the neck opening. Trim the seam allowance in half.

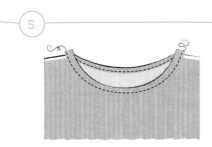

5

Fold the bias tape to the inside of the neck opening, tucking the seam allowance into the center of the tape. Fold again until all the tape is on the inside and only the dress fabric is showing around the neck. Stitch the tape to the neckline on the inside of the dress, as close to the outer fold as possible. This will also show as topstitching on the right side of the neckline.

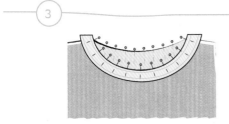

6

Fold one cuff piece in half and stitch the short ends together. Repeat with the other cuff piece. Press the seam allowance open.

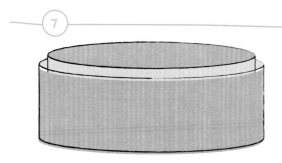

Fold the cuff pieces in half, wrong sides together, matching raw edges at the end opposite the fold. Press the fold flat.

Baste each sleeve hem at ⅜ in (1 cm) and ¾ in (2 cm), then gather to the cuff diameter. With the sleeves right side out, slip the cuff over the sleeve hem. Line up the raw edges, adjust the gathers, then pin and stitch. Remove the basting stitches, finish with a zigzag stitch through both layers at ⅜ in (1 cm), and trim.

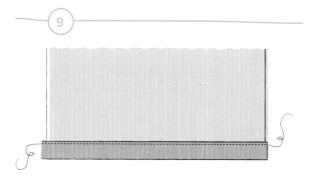

Press the hem of the dress up by ½ in (1.25 cm), wrong sides together, then press another ½ in (1.25 cm). Pin in place, then topstitch the hem as close to the inside fold as possible.

OTHER STYLES TO TRY

BUTTONS

Buttons don't always need buttonholes to be used in garment construction. Sewing a few buttons from your collection onto the front of a dress is a great way to showcase your favorites. Simply mark and sew a few buttons onto the dress in a spot you prefer. I like to add two or three buttons down the center front, just below the neckline.

RICKRACK TRIM

I think a little rickrack trim on a garment can up the vintage factor in a big way. Try adding it around the hem, neckline, or on the cuffs. It can be a fun little detail that is easy to sew! Find tips for sewing rickrack in Chapter 3 (page 131).

Like this style?
Check out the sleeveless sheath on page 72.

THE PLEATED SKIRT

Personally, I love a good pleat. It is a much more formal and polished way to create fullness in a garment, and when not in motion, the fabric hangs flat, unlike the pouf of a gather, making a smooth and flattering line.

Pleats are great because they look impressive, but they are incredibly easy to create by simply folding fabric. They offer a nice alternative to gathers and, for the most part, any spot that has gathers can usually become pleats and vice versa. I have made this version of a pleated skirt easier for the beginner sewer by including a simple elastic waistband.

Key characteristics
The main element of this skirt are the folds of fabric that create the pleats. The waistband has elastic, and from there the fullness of the folds fall down from the waist to the hem. This short version lands mid-thigh.

Who does it suit?
The pleats of the skirt will create volume for a larger hip, and the elastic waist will stretch to fit to either your natural waist or your hip, depending on where you would like to wear it. Keep in mind that this skirt is rather short, so be ready to bare some leg!

Suitable fabrics
Because the pleats will be pressed, it's easiest for a beginner to stick to natural fibers that will take to an iron easily, like cotton and linen. Also, due to the elastic waist, bulk is not a good idea, so I recommend looking for a quilt-weight cotton or similar fabric.

Styling tips
To downplay the sweetness of this skirt, try wearing it with a concert T-shirt, tights, and boots to give it a bit of a rocker edge. Alternatively, if you want to work the youthful angle, a cardigan and flats will look fresh and timeless.

MAKING A PLEATED SKIRT

YOU WILL NEED

- 2 yds (1.9 m) lightweight to medium-weight woven fabric, 60 in (150 cm) wide
- 1½ yds (1.4 m) elastic, ¾ in (2 cm) wide
- Thread

GETTING STARTED

Having a good iron is essential for all sewing, but especially for pressing pleats, so make sure yours is in working order before starting this project. Take your time with folding and pressing, being sure to press by lowering and lifting your iron, instead of moving the iron back and forth over the fabric. Simply press, lift, move, and press again.

PATTERN PIECES

1101 = skirt center front (cut 1 on fold)
1102 = skirt side front (cut 2)
1103 = skirt center back (cut 1 on fold)
1104 = skirt side back (cut 2)
1105 = waistband (cut 2 on fold)

TIP

You will be pinning and pressing your pleats, so only use glass-head pins or pins made entirely of metal so you do not accidently melt any plastic-head pins to your iron and new skirt!

Download your pattern here:
http://bit.ly/1q9FYTB

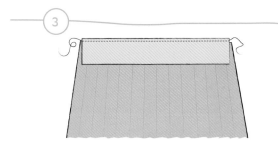

Sew the skirt side front pieces to the skirt center front. Then sew the skirt side back pieces to the skirt center back. Finish the seams at ⅜ in (1 cm) and trim excess seam allowance. Following the marks on the pattern, fold and pin the pleats in place around the entire skirt.

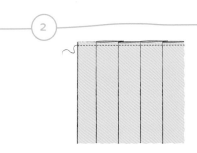

Baste the pleats in place at the ⅜-in (1-cm) seam allowance. (See the tutorial on page 21 for a reminder of working with pleats.)

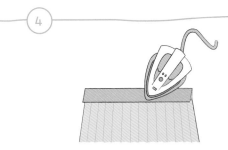

Place one waistband on top of one of the skirt pieces, right sides together. Stitch across the top, keeping the pleats in place. Repeat with the other waistband and skirt piece. Press the seam allowances up toward the waistband.

Fold and press the waistband toward the wrong side of the skirt so that there are 1½ in (4 cm) of waistband on the wrong side. This should cover the seam you have just sewn. Repeat on the other skirt and waistband piece.

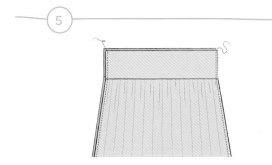

Unfold the waistband so it is open, and place the two skirt pieces right sides together. Sew along the side seams. Finish the seams with a zigzag stitch at ⅜ in (1 cm) and trim off the excess seam allowance. Press the seams flat.

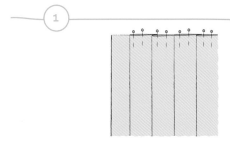

Zigzag around the raw top edge of the waistband to finish it.

Fold the waistband along the fold made in Step 4 and pin in place. Make sure the bottom of the waistband covers the seam with the skirt on the inside. Stitch on the waistband just above this seam, leaving a 2-in (5-cm) opening for inserting elastic into the waistband.

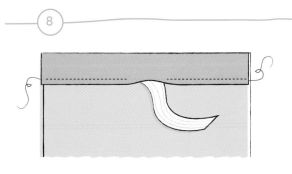

Cut a length of elastic to fit comfortably around your waist, plus 1 in (2.5 cm) for overlapping in the next step. Attach one end to a bodkin. Feed the bodkin and elastic into the opening left in the waistband. Feed around until the other end comes out of the opening.

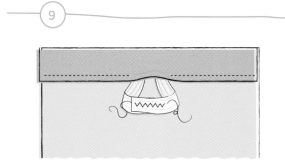

Overlap the ends by 1 in (2.5 cm) and stitch them together with a zigzag stitch. Go back and forth a few times with the stitch to secure the join before closing up the hole in the waistband with a straight stitch.

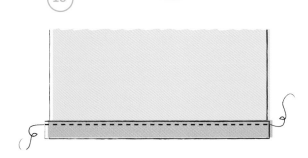

Press the hem of the skirt up by ½ in (1.25 cm), with wrong sides together. Press up another ½ in (1.25 cm) and pin in place. Topstitch the hem as close to the inside fold as possible.

OTHER STYLES TO TRY

GATHERED SKIRT

Love the idea of a cute short skirt, but not into making all those pleats? No problem. Simply follow the instructions on how to gather fabric on page 20 and gather the skirt front and back instead of pleating them. Continue with the instructions for the pleated version and you'll be all set!

SEWN-DOWN PLEATS

It is common practice to sew along the folds of pleats from the waist down to the point where you would like the fullness to begin. After Step 1, align your sewing machine needle just inside a pleat fold and topstitch it from the top of the skirt down about 3 in (7.5 cm) and backstitch. Repeat on all the pleats, then continue with the rest of the steps to finish the skirt.

Like this style?
Check out the tiered maxi skirt on page 42.

Opposite: African print cotton skirt by Solome Katongole (tl); Blue skirt by Topshop, styled by Jenna Richardson (bl); Stretch cotton skirt by La Redoute (r). **Above:** Hot pink skirt by ASOS, styled by Uli Chan (t); Navy textured skirt by BHS (b).

THE PENCIL SKIRT

I love the shape of a pencil skirt—it is one of those rare garments that is both business appropriate and sexy at the same time. The pencil skirt has been worn for decades, and still lives on as a classic choice today. It truly is a timeless shape.

While the ladies of the past might have worn their pencil skirts with suit jackets, these days this style of skirt looks just as comfortable paired with your favorite T-shirt or vintage pussy-bow blouse. It is always a good investment piece for your closet, and it's a rare garment that both grandmothers and granddaughters can agree on!

Key characteristics
The pencil skirt is the fitted cousin of the A-line skirt. Both are constructed in the same way, but the pencil skirt is a slimmer cut. It sits at the natural waist and follows the body to just above the knee.

Who does it suit?
This is not a skirt for the faint of heart—it is tailored and fitted, so there is nowhere to hide. It is best on a proportionate body, where there isn't a big difference between the hip and waist measurements. You can be big or small overall, but it would be hard to fit this skirt on a body with a large hip and a tiny waist.

Suitable fabrics
The pencil skirt can handle a medium-weight woven fabric really well, since there are no gathers or pleats to deal with. Cotton twill, cotton canvas, medium-weight linen, denim, and other similarly stable fabrics are all excellent choices.

Styling tips
This skirt is all about how you want to rock it. Personally, I love two pieces of clothing that are seemingly polar opposites, so try your skirt with a concert T-shirt and pumps. It would also look amazing with a fitted cardigan and kitten heels for a truly sexy retro look.

MAKING A PENCIL SKIRT

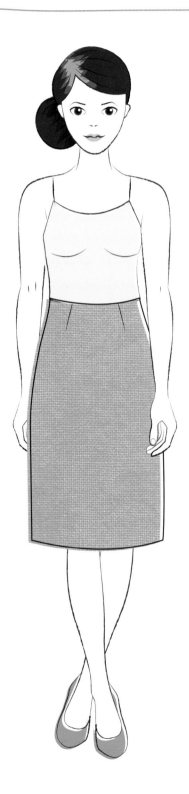

YOU WILL NEED

- 1⅞ yds (1.8 m) medium-weight woven fabric, 45 in (115 cm) wide
- 1⅛ yds (1 m) lightweight woven fusible interfacing, 18 in (46 cm) wide
- 9-in (23-cm) invisible zipper
- Thread

GETTING STARTED

If this is your first time installing a zipper, follow the tutorial on page 22 and try your hand on some scrap fabric before sewing on the finished skirt. This will boost your confidence before going on to the real thing, and you will be able to work out any mistakes on your test fabric.

PATTERN PIECES

1201 = skirt front (cut 1 on fold)
1202 = skirt back (cut 2)
1203 = waistband (cut 2 on fold)

TIP
Plan ahead and contact your local sewing machine dealer to get an invisible zipper foot for your specific machine. Not all feet fit all brands, so you might need to order it, and this is best done with a certified dealer for the brand of machine you own.

Download your pattern here:
http://bit.ly/1oWcbsk

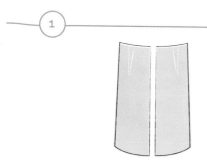

Sew the dart on one skirt back piece. Press it toward the center seam. Repeat with the other dart on the second back piece.

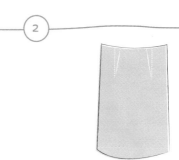

Sew the two darts on the skirt front piece and press them toward the center.

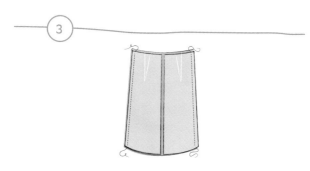

Place the skirt back pieces on top of the skirt front piece, right sides together, and line up the side seams. Sew the side seams from waist to hem. Press the seams open and finish the seams.

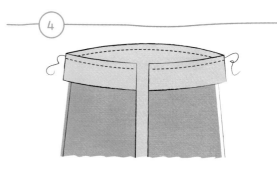

Place the glue side of the interfacing on one of the waistband pieces and press in place. This will be your outer waistband. Pin the waistband piece to the top of the skirt, right sides together, matching up the center notch and center back. Sew in place and press the seam allowance up toward the waistband.

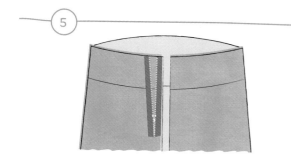

Finish the center back seam and line up the top of the zipper tape with the top of the waistband. Sew the invisible zipper into the center back seam, following the tutorial on page 22. Press the seam allowance open.

Turn and press the lower edge of the remaining waistband piece by ⅝ in (1.5 cm), with the wrong sides together.

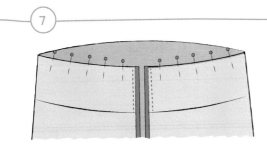

Pin this waistband piece to the skirt, right sides together, matching it with the waistband already sewn. Sew down along the zipper teeth on both sides of the skirt center back.

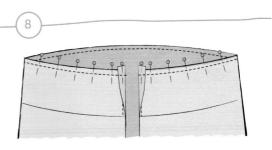

Fold the seam allowance and zipper away from the center back seam and pin. Sew the upper seam of the waistband, stitching over the top of the center back as folded.

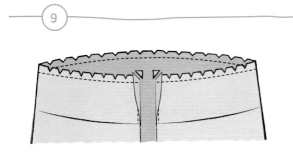

Trim the corners at the top of the zipper, and notch along the curve of the waistband. Understitch the waistband seam by sewing the seam allowance to the inside waistband, just inside the seam (see page 40).

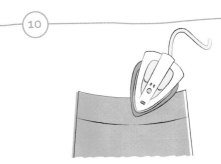

Turn the waistband right side out and press the top seam flat. Use a point turner to poke out the corner at the top of the zipper.

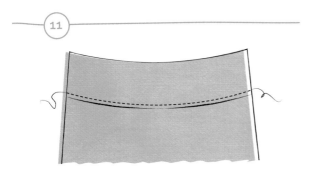

Pin the waistband in place. Topstitch the waistband to the skirt, stitching on the right side of the skirt, just above the seam where the skirt and the waistband meet.

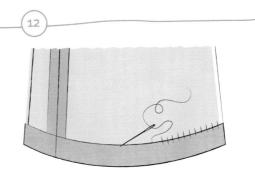

Fold up the hem by ½ in (1.5 cm) and press. Fold up another ½ in (1.5 cm) and press again. Stitch in place by machine, or sew in place with a hand stitch.

OTHER STYLES TO TRY

PLEATED HEM

An easy way to turn a classic pencil skirt into something fancier is to add a pleated hem. Measure the width of the front skirt, then add on half that number—if the width is 20 in (50 cm), the width of your ruffle will be 30 in (75 cm). The hem height can be anything you like, but make sure you add a ⅝-in (1.5-cm) seam allowance for sewing it to the dress, and 1 in (2.5 cm) for a double-fold hem at the bottom.

Cut two of these pieces, sew them right sides together along their side seams, then pleat them to fit the bottom hem of the skirt following the pleat tutorial on page 21. Sew the hem to the bottom of the skirt and you're done!

BACK SLIT

The version I have designed here doesn't have a slit up the back (a detail commonly found on pencil skirts), but it's easy to add if you'd like it. Simply sew down from the zipper to the desired top of the slit, then backstitch. Press each side of the seam allowance of the center back seam away from center and topstitch in place. Hem as instructed, folding up the slit. You can also follow these steps to create a slit on a side seam if you'd prefer your slit there.

Like this style?
Check out the A-line skirt on page 36.

THE UPCYCLED MEN'S SHIRT SKIRT

When looking for fabric to use for your next project, there's no need to limit yourself to new yardage when every thrift store has an abundance of men's dress shirts just waiting to be your next upcycled garment. These make a great blank canvas and can be turned into any number of new creations.

A quick and easy project is to make a simple skirt from a men's dress shirt, and the best part is that you don't even have to hem it! All the fancy detailing is done for you—all you have to do is turn it into an adorable new skirt for your wardrobe.

Key characteristics
There are endless upcycling projects using men's dress shirts, but this is a simple skirt with an elastic waist. The elastic gathers up the skirt, and the rest flows to the shirt's hem like a dirndl skirt. Because of the nature of the base garment, it will be rather short, ending above the knee.

Who does it suit?
This can suit anyone willing to wear a dirndl skirt—as long as you can find a shirt full enough to fit your hips. The shape works best for those with a smaller waist than hip.

Suitable fabrics
Men's shirts come in a variety of fabrics, but here it's best to stick to those made of actual shirting, usually found in stripes, solids, gingham, chambray, and other cotton or cotton/polyester blends. Steer clear of corduroy, flannel, and wool, as they will be too bulky for the elastic waist.

Styling tips
As with any upcycled garment, this will have a very casual feel, so play that up—don't try to make it what it's not. It's great with a shirt tucked in, topped with a belt, and will look so good that no one will guess it's an upcycle project!

Shirt skirt styled by Tasmin Roberts.

MAKING AN UPCYCLED MEN'S SHIRT SKIRT

YOU WILL NEED
- A men's dress shirt that is at least a few inches wider than your hip or waist, whichever is wider
- 1½ yds (1.4 m) elastic, ¾ in (2 cm) wide
- Thread

GETTING STARTED
The key to this project is finding the right shirt, so take your time and find one that is the right size and length to suit your body. Search the XL and XXL sizes so you have a lot of fabric to gather into the elastic waistband. Ideally your shirt will be 4–6 in (10–15 cm) wider than your widest point below your bust.

TIP
Before heading out to the thrift store, measure your waist and hip and write down those measurements. Take them with you to the store, along with a tape measure, so you can make sure the shirt you buy will work for your body!

1

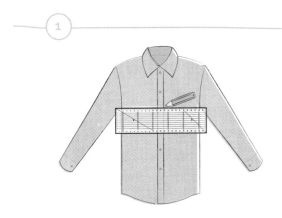

Straighten out your chosen shirt and lay it flat on a smooth surface. Use a water-soluble marking tool and ruler to draw a line across the chest of the shirt, directly under the sleeve.

2

Cut along that line with scissors, through both layers of the shirt. Make sure it doesn't move out of place. If necessary, pin the layers in place before cutting.

3

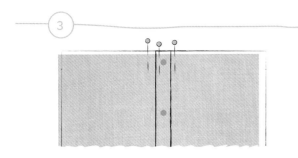

Secure the area along the button placket with pins to keep the layers of the placket in place.

4

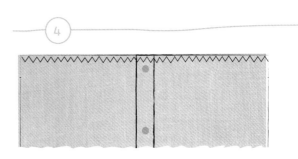

Finish the top edge around the shirt with a zigzag stitch. Sew it directly on the edge.

5

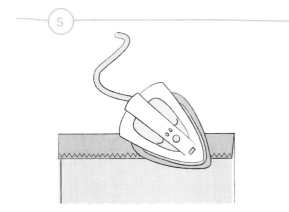

Fold the top of the shirt down 1 in (2.5 cm) and pin in place. Press with an iron.

6

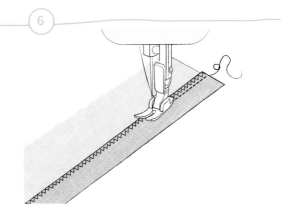

Stitch close to the zigzag edge, leaving an opening of 2 in (5 cm) for inserting elastic into the waist.

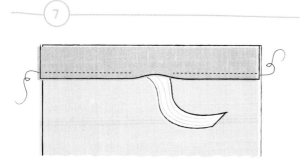

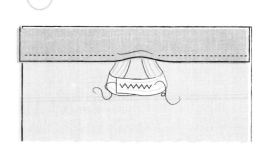

Cut a length of elastic to fit comfortably around your waist, plus an additional 1 in (2.5 cm) for overlapping. Attach a bodkin to one end. Insert the bodkin and elastic into the 2-in (5-cm) opening left in the top of the shirt.

Work the elastic around the shirt and pull both ends out of the opening. Overlap the elastic ends by 1 in (2.5 cm) and sew them together with a zigzag stitch. Go back and forth a few times to secure the join.

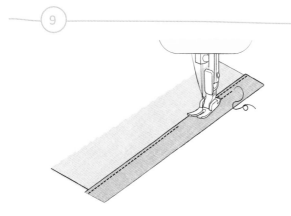

Fit the elastic back into the opening and close it up with a straight stitch.

OTHER STYLES TO TRY

CHANGE THE BUTTONS

Love the shirt you found for your skirt upcycle but hate the buttons? That is an easy fix! Take the shirt to your local fabric store and find buttons you prefer. Just make sure that they are the same size as the originals so they will fit in the buttonholes and keep your skirt closed.

STRAIGHTEN THE HEM

If a shirttail hem isn't for you, it is super easy to trim it down and make it a regular straight hem. Take your clear ruler and draw a line straight across the hem, then cut along the line. Fold the hem up by ½ in (1.25 cm) and press. Repeat with another ½-in (1.25-cm) fold and press again. Stitch close to the inside fold and your skirt is complete!

Like this style?
Check out the upcycled T-shirt dress on page 66.

THE WRAP SKIRT

One of my absolute favorite garments to make and teach is the wrap skirt. It is chic and retro-inspired, yet easy to make and flattering on everyone. It flexes up and down along with your waist as you gain and lose a few pounds, and all the while looks perfect.

Depending on the fabric you choose, this skirt can be clean and modern minimal, or it can be cutesy and vintage feminine. It really is a versatile garment and never goes out of style. Everyone from Mary Tyler Moore to Madonna has worn the wrap skirt, and it will live on for generations to come.

Key characteristics
Wrap skirts are usually either a big circle skirt, or use panels for a more A-line shape. This skirt is the latter, with a fitted skirt that sits up at your natural waist and an A-line skirt that pitches from the waist to the hem. There is an overlap, which I like to wear in the back, but you can also wear it in the front—either is correct.

Who does it suit?
As long as the overlap covers your body, this is for you! It is good on every body type and can easily be worn by women of all ages and tastes. This is a rare skirt that suits everyone.

Suitable fabrics
I suggest sticking to a lightweight to medium-weight woven fabric so the skirt can retain its A-line shape. If the fabric is too light it will be okay, but very loose and drapey. Cotton and linen woven fabrics like quilt weight, chambray, and twill are ideal choices.

Styling tips
I think a wrap skirt looks best with a fitted shirt that is tucked in, since the skirt is cinched and flat at the waist. It is a perfect way to show off a tiny waist! Try it with a shirt and cardigan, knee-high socks, and boots.

Opposite: Wrap skirt by Rip Curl, styled by Jenna Richardson
Above: Wrap skirt by Christine Haynes, styled by Elizabeth Russo. (t); Hawaiian print wrap skirt, styled by Jean Dotts (b).

MAKING A WRAP SKIRT

YOU WILL NEED

- 3¼ yds (2.75 m) lightweight to medium-weight fabric, 45 in (115 cm) wide
- 3 yds (2.75 m) double-fold bias tape
- Thread

GETTING STARTED

This project calls for a buttonhole to be sewn through the layers of the bias tape waistband. Practice a few on some scrap fabric, but make sure that the scrap closely represents the fabric you will sew through on the skirt so that it's an honest trial run. Read your sewing machine's manual if you have questions on how to use its buttonhole feature.

PATTERN PIECES

1301 = skirt front (cut 2)
1302 = skirt back (cut 2)

TIP

If you have trouble making bias tape by folding it manually and pressing, try one of the many bias tape makers out on the market. They might be a helpful time saver! Just make sure that all the folds are correct as you are no longer in control.

Download your pattern here:
http://bit.ly/1ygbiQl

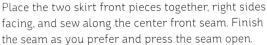

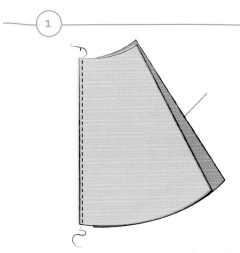

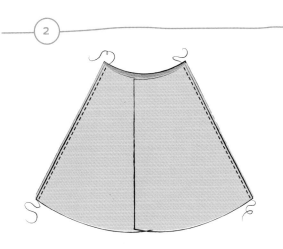

1

Place the two skirt front pieces together, right sides facing, and sew along the center front seam. Finish the seam as you prefer and press the seam open.

2

Place the skirt back pieces on top of the skirt front, right sides together, and sew along the two side seams. Finish the seams as you prefer and press open.

3

Press the two open back edges of the skirt ¼ in (0.7 cm) into the skirt, wrong sides together. Press another ¼ in (0.7 cm) and pin in place. Topstitch as close to the inside fold as possible through all layers.

4

Press up the hem of the skirt by ¼ in (0.7 cm), wrong sides together. Press another ¼ in (0.7 cm) and pin in place. Topstitch the hem as close to the inside fold as possible.

5

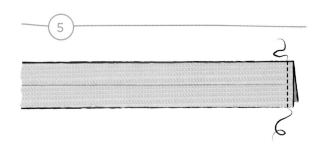

Cut a length of bias tape to match the length of the waist seam, plus enough to wrap around your body to tie the skirt closed. This can be as long or as short as you prefer. Open out the ends of the bias tape and fold them right sides together. Stitch them at ⅜ in (1 cm), then turn them right side out.

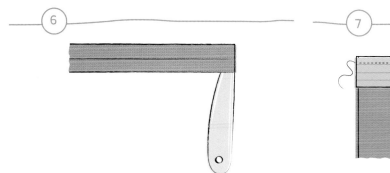

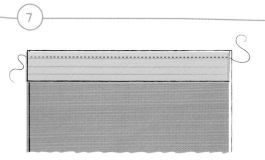

Use a point turner to form a crisp corner and refold the end of the bias tape along the original fold lines. Press flat.

Find the center of the bias tape and match it with the skirt center front. Open up the first fold on the tape and pin it to the skirt, right sides and raw edges together. Pin from the center front to the ends of the skirt in each direction, then stitch along the fold closest to the raw edge. Only sew the tape that is pinned to the skirt—do nothing yet with the ties that extend either end.

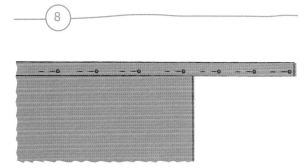

Fit the seam allowance into the center fold of the bias tape and fold half of the bias tape to the inside. Keep the remaining tape on the right side of the skirt so half is on the inside and half is on the outside. Pin in place.

Sew from one end of the tape to the other end, close to the inside edge of the tape, and closing up the fold on the tape as well as securing it to the skirt. Sew on the right side of the skirt so that you can see your topstitching, making sure you also catch the bias tape on the back.

The skirt can simply overlap and be worn as is. If you'd prefer to have a hole for the tie to feed through to the front of the skirt, mark a spot on the waistband with a water-soluble pen. Follow the buttonhole settings on your machine and sew a buttonhole in the waistband.

OTHER STYLES TO TRY

APPLIQUÉ

Play up the 1970s vibe and appliqué some fun shapes to the skirt. I have many vintage wrap skirts with all kinds of appliqué on them; everything from fruit, to boats, to images of the sun. Any shape you like can be sewn onto the skirt. Check out the tutorial on page 130.

CONTRAST BINDING

As with the wrap dress, the bias tape will be exposed when worn, so try making it out of a contrasting fabric to the body of the skirt. Anything with stripes will appear on the diagonal, so consider the bias in relation to the print when choosing a fabric for the bias tape. If you need a refresher, read the bias tape lesson on page 26.

Like this style?
Check out the wrap dress on page 90.

CHAPTER 3
TRIMS AND
EMBELLISHMENTS

Patch pockets   128
Shaped pockets   129
Appliqué   130
Lace and rickrack   131
Basic embroidery stitches   132

Opposite: Embroidered shift dress by La Redoute.

PATCH POCKETS

Not only are pockets cute, they are seriously functional. Adding a patch pocket to a garment is quick and easy, and you can place them just about anywhere. I have suggestions throughout the book for places to use them, but there's no need to limit yourself to my ideas. Make them from matching fabrics, contrasting fabrics, or embellish them and then place them wherever you like!

1

Measure the size pocket you want, then add ⅝ in (1.5 cm) to each side, ⅝ in (1.5 cm) to the bottom, and 1 in (2.5 cm) to the top. Cut out the pocket from fabric. Finish all four sides of the pocket with a zigzag stitch on the edge of the fabric.

2

Fold the top of the pocket down 1 in (2.5 cm), right sides together, and pin in place. Important: Resist the temptation to press this fold! It will later be turned right side out, so leaving it unpressed now will make this much easier.

3

Stitch from the top fold to the bottom of the fold on the sides at the ⅝-in (1.5-cm) seam allowance. Be sure to backstitch at the top and bottom.

4

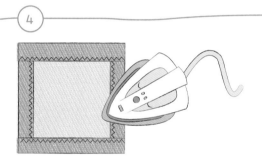

Turn the top right side out and use a point turner to form perfect top corners. Then fold the sides under by ⅝ in (1.5 cm) and press. Fold the bottom up by ⅝ in (1.5 cm) and press.

5

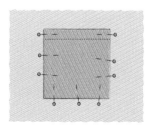

Stitch across the bottom of the top flap to hold it in place inside the pocket. Pin the pocket in position on your garment.

6

Stitch around the pocket sides and bottom, pivoting at each bottom corner and securing the start and end of the stitch with a backstitch.

SHAPED POCKETS

A shaped pocket is a patch pocket, but in a shape other than a square or rectangle with straight sides and right angles. Since it is very hard to get a curve perfect by simply folding in the sides, this kind of pocket needs to be made in a slightly different way. Follow along, though, and you'll see how easy it is!

1

Draw the shape you want for your pocket and cut two identical shapes for one pocket.

2

Place the shapes right sides together and sew around them, leaving a 2-in (5-cm) opening on one side. If there is a straight edge anywhere on the shape, pick that spot to leave open.

3

Trim the seam allowance down to ⅛ in (0.3 cm) around the shape, except for where the opening is located.

4

Turn the shape right sides out and use your point turner to poke out any angles and curves. Fold the seam allowance into the opening and then press the whole shape flat.

5

Topstitch around the entire shape, close to the edge, and close up the opening at the same time.

6

Place the shape where you want it to sit on the garment, and pin it in place.

7

Sew on top of your stitching to secure the shape to your garment. Be sure to leave the top edge open so it will function as a pocket!

APPLIQUÉ

Learning to appliqué is incredibly easy and can really change the look and feel of a classic shape. I have a wrap skirt in my closet that has some appliquéd strawberries connected with rickrack "stems" that is just so adorable. If you can sew a zigzag stitch, you can appliqué, so get thinking about what you want to adorn your next creation with!

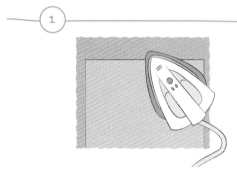

Fuse some interfacing to the wrong side of your fabric. This will stiffen the fabric a little bit, making it easier to sew. I like to use lightweight woven fusible interfacing, but any fusible kind will work.

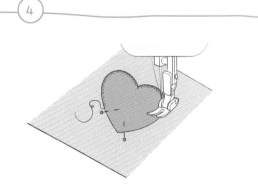

Set your machine to a wide and short zigzag stitch so that the threads of the stitch land on either side of the edge of the fabric, with almost no distance between each stitch.

Cut out your shape from the fabric and interfacing.

Pin the shape to the garment or accessory you wish to sew it to.

Give the whole unit a press of the iron and you're done!

LACE AND RICKRACK

Sewing on a lace or rickrack trim can turn an otherwise simple garment into something unique. Lace adds an elegant touch, and is very easy to sew onto a hem, or in the middle of a garment. I know rickrack isn't for everyone, but I love its retro flare, and in the right place it can look really striking. It comes in a wide range of colors and widths, so search the Internet for some fun options.

LACE HEM

Before attaching the lace, finish your hem as instructed for your project. Pin the lace to the hem so that most of the lace hangs below the hem, but the top portion covers any hem stitching.

Set your machine to a zigzag stitch with medium length and width, and select a thread that matches the color of the lace as closely as possible. Sew a zigzag stitch right on top of the hem.

LACE TRIM

Pin the lace where you'd like it to be on your garment. Set your machine to a zigzag stitch with medium length and width, and choose a thread that matches the lace as closely as possible. Sew a zigzag stitch on the top and bottom of the lace.

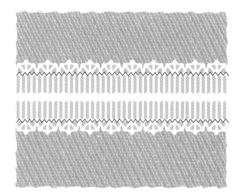

RICKRACK

Pin the rickrack in place on your garment. Set your machine to a regular straight stitch, and select a thread that matches the color of your rickrack as closely as possible. Simply sew and pivot with each scallop of the rickrack to secure it in place.

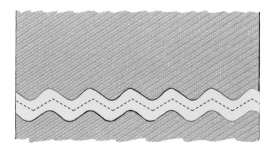

BASIC EMBROIDERY STITCHES

Embroidery is basically drawing with thread. I love looking at my garments the way an artist looks at a blank canvas; endless possibilities for customization and self-expression. It takes very little equipment—just a needle, some floss, and a hoop to keep the fabric firm.

BACKSTITCH

The backstitch is like a line that can be made into anything. Draw whatever you like, write a message—whatever your heart desires.

Cut a length of floss from fingertips to elbow. Knot the end and thread it through an embroidery needle. Pass the needle through the fabric from back to front, then insert it just to the right of this point. Pass under the thread, and emerge on the other side. Keep the distance from thread to needle equal on either side.

Pull the needle to form a stitch. Repeat by inserting the needle just to the left of the first stitch, pass under the thread, and come out with your needle on the other side. Again, keep the stitches equal in length and make sure there is no gap between them so that you create one continuous line.

RUNNING STITCH

The running stitch is similar to the backstitch, except there are gaps between each stitch so the finished result is like a dashed line.

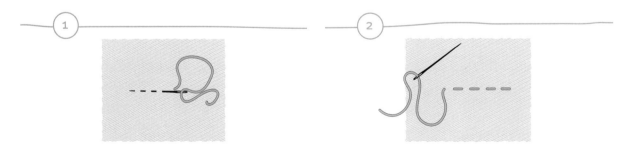

Go through the fabric from back to front. Insert the needle just to the left, then emerge and repeat.

Now pull the needle all the way through to create a few stitches at once. Keep your stitches an equal length.

SATIN STITCH

If you are looking to fill in areas of a design or cover a lot of ground, the satin stitch is the right choice. It's a simple up and down or side-to-side stitch that can make a big impact.

①

Cut a length of floss from fingertips to elbow. Knot the end and thread it through the eye of an embroidery needle. Go through the fabric from the back to the front. Just to the side of the thread, insert the needle and bring it out immediately below the original emergence point so there is no gap between them.

Pull the needle through and repeat with the threads right against each other so it looks like a solid block of color. The stitches can be used to fill various shapes.

SEED STITCH

I took a semester in college for embroidery and fell in love with the seed stitch. It's simple and imperfect and can be wonderfully abstract.

①

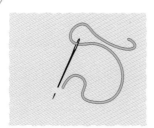

②

Cut a length of floss from fingertips to elbow. Knot the end and thread it through the eye of an embroidery needle. Go through the fabric from the back to the front. Just next to the thread, insert the needle and come up through the fabric only a small distance away.

Pull the needle through the fabric and that is your first seed stitch. Continue by making a pattern or any abstract creation.

CHAPTER 4
RESOURCES

Useful websites   136
Glossary   138
Contributor index   140

Opposite: Vintage hand-beaded kaftan, styled by Giovanna Scarfo.

USEFUL WEBSITES

SEWING BLOGS

Burda Style
www.BurdaStyle.com

City Stitching with Christine Haynes
www.christinehaynes.blogspot.com

Colette Patterns' Coletterie
www.coletterie.com

Craftsy
www.craftsy.com/blog

Flossie Teacakes
flossieteacakes.blogspot.com

Gertie's New Blog for Better Sewing
www.blogforbettersewing.com

Grainline Studio
grainlinestudio.com

House of Pinheiro
houseofpinheiro.blogspot.com

Kollabora
www.kollabora.com

Miss Make
www.missmake.com

Noodlehead
www.noodle-head.com

Oona Balloona
www.oonaballoona.com

Paunnet
www.paunnet.com

Sew Convert
sewconvert.wordpress.com

Sew Mama Sew
www.sewmamasew.com

Tilly and the Buttons
www.tillyandthebuttons.com

INDIE PATTERN DESIGNERS

Aime Comme Marie Patterns
www.aimecommemarie.com

By Hand London
byhandlondon.com

Christine Haynes Patterns
www.ChristineHaynes.com

Colette Patterns
www.colettepatterns.com

Grainline Studio
shop.grainlinestudio.com

Green Bee Patterns
greenbeepatterns.bigcartel.com

Made by Rae
www.made-by-rae.com

Megan Nielsen
megannielsen.com

Merchant & Mills
merchantandmills.com

Named
www.namedclothing.com

Ohhh Lulu
www.ohhhlulu.com

Papercut Patterns
papercutpatterns.com

Pauline Alice
www.paulinealice.com

République du Chiffon
republiqueduchiffon.com

Salme Sewing Patterns
www.salmesewingpatterns.com

Sew Liberated Patterns
www.sewliberated.com

Sewaholic Patterns
www.sewaholicpatterns.com

Thread Theory Designs
threadtheory.ca

Tilly and the Buttons
shop.tillyandthebuttons.com

Victory Patterns
www.victorypatterns.com

FABRIC SITES

USA
A Fashionable Stitch
shop.afashionablestitch.com

Britex Fabrics
www.britexfabrics.com

Drygoods Design
www.drygoodsdesignonline.com

The Needle Shop
www.theneedleshop.net

Pink Castle Fabrics
www.pinkcastlefabrics.com

Pink Chalk Fabrics
www.pinkchalkfabrics.com

Purl Soho
www.purlsoho.com

Superbuzzy
superbuzzy.com

UK
Backstitch
www.backstitch.co.uk

Gutherie & Ghani
www.gutherie-ghani.co.uk

Ray Stitch
www.raystitch.co.uk

Sewbox
www.sewbox.co.uk

The Village Haberdashery
www.thevillagehaberdashery.co.uk

France
Atelier Brunette
atelierbrunette.com

Japan
Miss Matatabi
www.missmatatabi.com

Italy
Super Cut
supercut.it

Spain
Telaria
telaria.es

GLOSSARY

Backstitch Sewing forward, then back, at the beginning and end of a line of stitching in order to prevent it from unraveling.

Basting stitch A temporary stitch, longer than average, to hold fabric in place while stitching. This is usually removed after sewing a final stitch.

Bias The diagonal angle across the grain of the fabric.

Bias tape A strip of fabric cut on the bias, typically used for finishing openings.

Bodice The top half of a dress, from the shoulders to the waist.

Bodkin A pair of tweezers with a stopper that clamps and locks on elastic or a drawstring for threading through casings.

Casing A fold that is stitched down and filled with elastic or drawstring, as on the waist of pants or skirts.

Clipping To reduce bulk on a corner, or for an inner curve to lay flat, the seam allowance is cut on the inside of the seam.

Crossgrain (weft) The width of a fabric, from selvage to selvage.

Dart A fold in the fabric to shape a garment around the body's curves.

Ease The distance from the body to the garment, allowing for movement. Each pattern's ease is based on the garment's style.

Ease stitching Used to fit a wider piece of fabric into a smaller piece of fabric, without any puckering, gathers, or pleats in the seam.

Elastic thread A thin, round elastic cord used in the bobbin for shirring fabric.

Facing A piece of fabric that is sewn to an edge and turned to the inside for a finished seam.

French seam A seam that is first sewn wrong sides together, and then turned inward and sewn again to enclose any raw edges.

Gathering Reducing a larger piece of fabric to fit a smaller piece of fabric, with small, deliberate folds sewn into the seam.

Grainline To put a pattern piece "on grain" is to match the grainline with the lengthwise grain on the fabric.

Hem The bottom of any part of the garment (sleeve, pant leg, skirt, dress) that is usually folded and sewn.

Interfacing A fabric used in areas requiring additional stability, such as collars and cuffs.

Invisible zipper A zipper that is completely hidden in a seam.

Lengthwise grain (warp) The length of the fabric, from cut end to cut end.

Lining An identical layer of fabric on the inside of a garment, meant to provide opacity.

Muslin Inexpensive cotton—available bleached or unbleached—typically used to sew a practice garment to test fit.

Notch Marks on the pattern piece that indicate where the pieces are to line up. Also refers to a way of cutting an outer curve so it will lay flat.

Notions All the items required to sew a project, with exception of the pattern and fabric.

Pinking shears A pair of scissors with a row of teeth on the blade that cut the fabric into small triangular points. Most fabrics will not fray when cut with pinking shears.

Pivot To sink the needle into the fabric, lift the presser foot, turn the fabric, lower the foot, and resume stitching. Typically used on corners.

Pleat A fold in the fabric to provide fullness.

Press Placing an iron on the project and applying heat and pressure, but without the back-and-forth motions of ironing.

Regular zipper A zipper with exposed teeth and pull.

Right side The outer side of the fabric that you want seen when finished.

Right sides together Placing two pieces of fabric together, with the outer sides of the fabric facing each other. This is how most seams are sewn.

Seam The place where two or more pieces of fabric are sewn together.

Seam allowance The distance from the stitch line to the edge of the fabric.

Seam ripper A tool with a point and a sharp beveled U, meant for cutting and breaking stitches.

Selvage The two uncut sides of fabric, finished in the manufacturing. The crossgrain threads go from selvage to selvage.

Serger Also known as an overlock machine, these use cone thread and sew the seam, cut off the seam allowance, and finish the seam all at once.

Shirring Gathering fabric with elastic thread so it remains stretchy.

Staystitch A stabilizing stitch that helps prevent stretching on curves while sewing.

Straight stitch A basic stitch that moves forward in only one direction.

Topstitch Exposed stitching on the outside of a project or garment.

Understitch To sew the seam allowance to a facing or lining, which is meant to help the facing or lining stay to the inside of the garment.

Wrong side The side of the fabric that you do not want seen as you wear it.

Wrong sides together Placing two pieces of fabric together with the inside of the fabric face to face and the outer (right sides) on the outside.

Zigzag stitch A stitch that moves forward as well as side to side, commonly used for finishing seams.

CONTRIBUTOR INDEX

BLOGGERS AND MAKERS

Kayley Anne
www.sidewalkready.com

Anami and Janine
www.anamiandjanine.com
sales@anamiandjanine.com

Christine Battaglia
www.workmywardrobe.com
blockandbattaglia@gmail.com

Karine Bono
www.karinebono.co.uk
karinebono@live.com

Nancy Dee Brooke (Nancy Dee Clothing)
www.nancydee.co.uk

Uli Chan
ulimali.blogspot.com

Jean Dotts (Bop and Awe)
www.etsy.com/shop/bopandawe

Dressabelle
www.dressabelle.com.sg

Chie Duncan (Vivat Veritas)
www.vivatveritas.com

Solome Katongole
www. solomekatongole.com

Emily Lane Style
www.emilylanestyle.com

Sakura Masada
www.mango—mochi.blogspot.com

Macailah Maxwell
www.takealovelylook.com

Giovanna Scarfo (Dusty Petals)
dustypetals.com.au

Kelly Stiles (Wildlife Vintage)
www.etsy.com/shop/WildLifeTX

Lauren Taylor (LLADYBIRD)
lladybird.com

Merrick White (Merrick's Art)
www.merricksart.com

Keren Zarka (Anna K.)
www.etsy.com/uk/shop/ANNAKSHOP

With special thanks to
American Apparel
ASOS
BHS
Daxon
Dunnes Stores
EAST
F&F
Free People
Bex Hawkins
La Redoute
M&Co
Miss Selfridge
Oh My Love
Pachamama Bali
PeopleTree
Esther Richardson
Jenna Richardson
Tasmin Roberts
Elizabeth Rosso
Rip Curl
Topshop
Wallis
Warehouse

PHOTOGRAPHERS

Mandy Chua (ASOS skirt, page 108)
dancinghammy@gmail.com

Paul Hance (Solome Katongole, pages 72, 78, and 108)
www.paulhancephotography.com

Kai Heeringa (baby doll dress, page 60; Tailor and Stylist
skirt, page 78)
kaiheeringaphotography.com

Jeremy Khoo (Dressabelle dress, page 96)
www.dressabelle.com.sg

Angela Rekucki (American Apparel skirt, page 78)
lotsapresence@gmail.com

Will Robb Photography (Chie Duncan dress, page 60)
www.willrobbphotography.com
wgkrobb@gmail.com

Philip White (Merrick White mod dress, page 96)
www.merricksart.com

INDEX

A-line skirts 30, 36–41
appliqué 130
assembling 8, 10
auto sizing/scaling 8

baby doll dresses 11, 30, 60–65
back slits 113
backstitch 16, 132, 138
basics 12–33
basting stitch 14, 20, 50, 138
bias 92, 138
bias tape 26–27, 62, 74, 80,
    83, 86, 92, 95, 98, 122, 125, 138
blogs 28, 136, 140
blousy bodices 59
bobbins 16, 56
bodices 55, 59, 138
bodkins 15, 138
border prints 83
bottom ruffles 59
bracket lines 10–11
bust measurements 28
buttons 16, 25, 101, 119

casing 138
chalk pencils 15
chambray cotton 91, 115, 121
circle skirts 31, 78–83
clipping 138
color blocking 53
contour darts 19
contrast 41, 47, 83, 95, 125
contributors 140–141
corduroy 37, 115
cotton 15, 37, 49, 55, 61, 67, 73, 85, 91,
    97, 103, 109, 115, 121
cotton gauze 43
crewel needles 15
crossgrain 138
cuffs 98
cutting out 10–11

darts 15, 18–19, 138
denim 109

designers 136–137
double gauze 49
downloads 8
drape 10, 43, 49, 67
dressmaker's shears 14

ease 28, 138
elastic thread 55–59, 138
embroidery 53, 95, 132–133
eyelet trim 77

fabric cutting 10–11
fabric websites 137
fabric widths 10, 30–33
facings 138
feed dogs 16
flannel 115
folds 10–11, 18
foot pedals 16
foot plates 16

gathering 20, 50, 62, 107, 138
gingham 115
glossary 138–139
grainlines 10–11, 138
guidelines 10

hand sewing 15, 25
hand wheels 16
hems 25, 89, 113, 119, 131, 138
hip measurements 28, 116

interfacing 30, 138
ironing boards 15
irons 15

kimono sleeves 91
knife pleats 21

lace 65, 77, 89, 131
lace hems 131
lawn 43, 49, 85
lengthwise grain 10, 138
linen 37, 73, 91, 97, 103, 109, 121

linings 138
lycra 67

makers 140
manuals 16
maxi skirts 31, 42–47
measurements 10, 15, 28–29, 116
men's shirt skirts 114–119
milliner's needles 15
mistakes 7
muslin 28, 38, 138

needles 15
notches 40, 112, 138
notions 138

ombre effect 47

paper scissors 14
patch pockets 65, 71, 128
pattern cutting 10–11
pattern designers 136–137
pattern files 8
pattern layouts 30–33
PDF downloads 8
pencil skirts 30, 108–113
pinking shears 138
pins 14, 104
pivoting 138
pleated skirts 31, 102–107
pleats 21, 104, 107, 113, 139
pockets 65, 71, 128–129
point turners 15
polyester 15
presser feet 16
pressing 15, 104, 139
pressing hams 15
prewashing fabric 10
print mixing 47
printing 8

QR codes 8–9

raglan sleeves 49
rayon 15, 43, 49, 61, 67, 85
reprintable patterns 8
resources 134–141
retro embroidery 95
reverse buttons 16
rickrack 65, 101, 131
right sides 8, 139
right sides together 139
ruffles 59
rulers 14–15
running stitch 132

satin stitch 133
scissors 14
seam allowances 44, 139
seam finishing 24, 139
seam gauges 15
seam rippers 14, 139
seams 139
seed stitch 133
selvage 10–11, 139
sergers 139
sewing machines 15–16, 110
sewn-down pleats 107
shaped pockets 129
sharps 15
shears 14, 138
sheath dresses 33, 72–77
shift dresses 33, 96–101
shirring 55–59, 139
silk 15, 43, 49, 61, 67, 73, 85
simple darts 18
sizing 10, 28–29
sleeveless sheath dresses 33, 72–77
slip dresses 33, 84–89
smocked sundresses 32, 54–59
software 8
spool pins 16
staystitch 139
stitch length 16
stitch selection 16
stitch width 16

straight stitch 139
sundresses 32, 54–59, 89
Swiss dot 85
synthetic fabrics 15

T-shirt dresses 66–71
tank dresses 71
tape measures 15, 28, 116
techniques 18–27
test prints 8
test squares 8
thread 15
tiered maxi skirts 31, 42–47
tools 14–17
topstitch 41, 139
trims 126–133
tunic dresses 33, 48–53
twill 109, 121
two-sided arrows 10–11

understitch 139
upcycled men's shirt skirts 114–119
upcycled T-shirt dresses 66–71
URL links 8
useful addresses 136–137

vintage trim 77
voile 43, 49, 55, 73, 85, 97

waist measurements 28, 116
waistbands 41
warp 138
websites 136–137, 140–141
weft 138
wool 37, 115
wrap dresses 32, 90–95
wrap skirts 32, 120–125
wrong sides 139
wrong sides together 139

yoke embroidery 53

zigzag stitch 24, 139
zippers 22–23, 110